THE SCHOLL CASE

Anja Reich-Osang, a native of Berlin, has written for *Die Zeit*, *Die Welt* and *Berliner Zeitung*. In 2011, she and her husband published the book *Where Were You? A September Day in New York*, in which they recall their experiences of 9/11 while living in New York City. She was awarded the German Reporter Prize in 2012 and is currently working as senior editor at *Berliner Zeitung*. She lives in Berlin with her husband and her two children.

Imogen Taylor is a literary translator based in Berlin. Her translations include Sascha Arango's *The Truth and Other Lies* and Melanie Raabe's *The Trap*.

THE SCHOLL CASE

THE DEADLY END OF A MARRIAGE

ANJA REICH-OSANG

*Translated from the German
by Imogen Taylor*

TEXT PUBLISHING MELBOURNE AUSTRALIA

textpublishing.com.au

The Text Publishing Company
Swann House, 22 William Street, Melbourne, Victoria 3000, Australia

The Text Publishing Company (UK) Ltd
130 Wood Street, London EC2V 6DL, United Kingdom

First published in Germany as *Der Fall Scholl* by Ullstein extra Verlag, 2014
Copyright © Ullstein Buchverlage GmbH, Berlin
First published in English by The Text Publishing Company, 2016

Book design by Jessica Horrocks
Typeset by J&M Typesetting

Printed in Australia by Griffin Press, an Accredited ISO AS/NZS 14001:2004 Environmental Management System printer

National Library of Australia Cataloguing-in-Publication entry
Creator: Reich-Osang, Anja, author.
Title: The Scholl case: the deadly end of a marriage/by Anja Reich-Osang; translated from the German by Imogen Taylor.
ISBN: 9781925240931 (paperback)
ISBN: 9781922253552 (ebook)
Subjects: Scholl, Brigitte. Scholl, Heinrich. True crime stories—Germany—Berlin. Murder—Investigation—Germany—Berlin.
Other Creators/Contributors: Taylor, Imogen, translator.
Dewey Number: 364.1523092

For Alexander

CONTENTS

AUTHOR'S NOTE

This book tells a true story. It was written between October 2012 and March 2014 and is based on observations made during an eight-month trial and on interviews with friends and relations of the victim and the defendant, with the defendant's business partners, politician friends and lawyers, and with others who were able to provide information about Brigitte and Heinrich Scholl. Most of the people mentioned in this book bear their real names, but in a few cases they have had to be given pseudonyms. These are marked with an asterisk.

I also had several long talks with Heinrich Scholl himself, in the visitors' room of the prison in which he was serving his sentence. Over the course of those visits, Scholl wrote down and sent me the memories of his life. My last conversation with him took place in February 2015.

I would like to thank everyone who supported me in my work on this book.

—ANJA REICH-OSANG

PROLOGUE

On a summer's evening in Berlin, Heinrich Scholl's letters blew out of the window. They were on my desk; the last letter, which had come that day, was lying on top. In it, Scholl told of his day-to-day life in prison, which of his friends and relations still visited him, which kept their distance, what he was reading. Three closely written pages—and then a fourth, headed 'Power of Attorney'. Heinrich Scholl agreed to let me conduct research about him; he asked the local authorities, his lawyers and his friends to assist me in the work on my book. I had persuaded him. At last! I rang a friend and told her there was cause for celebration. When I left the house, the sun was shining and there was no wind. I left the window open a crack.

The first drops fell just as I was setting off for home. The rain grew heavier, the wind got up. I ran home, up the stairs, into the flat. Too late. The gale had flung open the window and wreaked havoc in my study, like an angry guest. I crawled about the floor, gathering up the pages. They were all there. Almost all. The last letter was missing, the one with the power of attorney. Of course. I looked at the window and imagined the closely written pages, covered in Scholl's sloping handwriting, sailing past my neighbours' windows into the summer night's storm—and with them my story, my book. I am not superstitious, but at that moment I was convinced it was a sign.

It was a day in August. Like so many days that summer, I had spent it in Ludwigsfelde, a small town to the south of Berlin where, three years before, a hideous crime had taken place. A woman had been brutally murdered in the woods, and her husband—the town's former mayor and a highly respected social democrat—had been arrested on suspicion of the crime.

I found myself at the trial as a reporter. Back then, in October 2012, everyone was talking about Heinrich Scholl— in Ludwigsfelde, in Brandenburg, in Berlin. The mayor who had killed his wife. A politician couldn't lose more face than that. I had only meant to sit in on a few days of the hearing, but I kept coming back. I had to; the story had a hold over me. I wanted to know whether or not he'd done it, of course. But above all, I realised that more was at stake here than murder.

Heinrich Scholl had assembled trucks in the Ludwigs-felde automobile works and made chairs for East Germany's state circus. When the Wall fell, he became involved in local politics, helping to found social democracy in Brandenburg, and was soon one of the most successful politicians of the new federal states. Like the country, he reinvented himself. His life seemed symbolic—proof that German unity was working. But what price did he pay for his ascent? What temptations did he withstand—or fail to withstand? And what had happened to his marriage in the almost twenty years in which he transformed Ludwigsfelde into a flourishing place of business?

On a folding chair in Potsdam Criminal Court, I sat between friends of the Scholls and citizens of Ludwigsfelde who couldn't believe that their mayor was a murderer and his marriage a farce. There were no eyewitnesses to the murder, hardly any clues and no proof, so the court summoned more and more witnesses. Half the town was called to testify: the Scholls' son, their neighbours, their cleaning lady, a beautician, the victim's best friends, the duty policeman, the doctor on call, a cyclist, the Macedonian landlord of Scholl's favourite Italian restaurant, a fellow party member, business friends, Scholl's tax advisor, a driving instructor, a former lover of the deceased, a singing florist and a Thai sex worker. They talked of love, power and the times they lived in. They were the dramatis personae of a historical era.

Only one person did not speak: Heinrich Scholl himself. For eight months he sat in the dock without saying a word, without answering a single question. I gave it a go all the same; on the day of the verdict I wrote him a letter asking whether I might visit him. A week later an envelope appeared in my letterbox. Return address: H. Scholl, Brandenburg an der Havel. He suggested a date.

I visited Heinrich Scholl in prison many times after that. He told me about his life—about his marriage. Sometimes he was quiet, sometimes exuberant; often he would cry.

Every time he protested his innocence. Sitting opposite him at the little table in the windowless visitors' cell, I believed him, but as soon as I was in my car, driving back to Berlin, I began to have my doubts. Wasn't he just an extremely skilful dodger? Hadn't he had all that time in his cell to think up answers to tricky questions? And if so, did he lie consciously? Or was he suppressing the truth because it was so awful that he would never be able to admit it to himself?

To begin with, not even his lawyers were allowed to know of my visits. They had proceeded to appeal after the verdict and were afraid their client might make some ill-considered remark. Scholl asked me not to publish anything about the appeal decision. He trusted me. Maybe because he had seen me in the courtroom every day of the hearing. Maybe because, like him, I came from East Germany. Maybe because I was a woman. Heinrich Scholl likes women, but he finds them hard to gauge. That was always his problem, his weakness. He didn't notice that his wife humiliated him for decades or that his Thai girlfriend, a sex worker, exploited him. Even now, in prison, he described his marriage as a picture of harmony and tried to persuade me that his relationship with the Thai woman had been something very special.

It is one of the strange certitudes of this story that this weakness, which led to the breakdown of Heinrich Scholl's marriage and—in all probability—to the murder of his wife, also ended up making my book possible.

Four hours were the extent of Heinrich Scholl's monthly

visiting hours. That wasn't much. And so, from his cell, he put together little groups of visitors and organised car pools. I was put on a list with a friend of his who was an asparagus farmer, along with his estate agent and his tax advisor. If my fellow car-pool drivers couldn't make it, they would ring up and send warm regards to 'Heiner'. When I wasn't in prison, I was drinking coffee in Ludwigsfelde with Brigitte Scholl's customers, eating crumble cake with her first boyfriend, standing at her grave with her best friend, walking through the woods of the Mark of Brandenburg with the policeman who had issued the missing person report, or dropping into Scholl's favourite restaurant, Da Toni's. At the end of an interview, Scholl's childhood friend Dieter Fahle, a former glassblower, gave me vases he had made himself. His cousin gave me fresh tomatoes from her garden. A business friend who was well up in Berlin's Thai underworld welcomed me outside a nightclub-cum-brothel with the words: 'First names only in there.'

I got regular letters from Brandenburg an der Havel; Heinrich Scholl had begun to record his life for me. It did him good, he said. On the back of the envelope he gave only his name, the street and the town, as if the prison were his private address and he the homeowner. On one occasion he sent a card showing a prisoner in a striped suit, staring help-lessly at a wall with clenched fists; another time he decorated his letter with dried flowers he had picked in the prison yard and pressed himself. He signed off 'Yours, Heinrich Scholl' and sent warm regards to my family.

A few months before, on my folding chair in the criminal court, I had wanted to get closer to this silent, mysterious man. Now he was almost too close to me. At night I would wake with a start after dreaming about wandering through the pinewoods of Brandenburg or standing like Clarice Starling in Hannibal Lecter's cell and hearing the door click shut behind me. When I woke, I would construct chains of circumstantial evidence in every possible permutation, and think of Truman Capote, who made friends with a murderer while working on *In Cold Blood*, his book about the murder of a Kansas farmer and his family. It was my favourite book: at once an example and a warning. And on that stormy summer's evening in Berlin, I decided it was time to stop, time to get away.

I ran down the stairs to the courtyard. It was still raining; lightning and thunder were alternating in quick succession as if the world was exploding. The pages were scattered over the entire courtyard; I found them behind the dustbins and in the bushes, gathered them up, dried them and flattened them. Everything was there, even the power of attorney.

Then I conducted the final interviews, attended Brigitte Scholl's class reunion and drove one last time to see Heinrich Scholl in prison. This time I spoke to him alone, three days in a row, over several hours. Then I wrote up the tapes and began to piece together what I had found out about him and Brigitte Scholl: the story of a man and a woman bound in love and hate and unable to part from one another.

THE LAST DAY

Brigitte Scholl disappeared on 29 December 2011, the day after her forty-seventh wedding anniversary. The flowers her husband had given her—red roses—were still on the living-room table; in the corner stood the Christmas tree, straight as a die and lavishly decorated. Everything had to be just so.

It was to be perfect, right up to the end.

Brigitte Scholl was sixty-seven years old and a beautician by trade. Her beauty salon was on the ground floor of their house. She was never unpunctual, never unfriendly; you never heard a loud word at the Scholls'. Their marriage was said to be irreproachable. When the first customer rang the bell at eight in the morning, Brigitte Scholl would be standing at the door in her white coat, her hair tied back. From the kitchen there'd be a good morning from her husband, the former mayor.

Heinrich Scholl was a legend in Ludwigsfelde. He had helped found social democracy there when the Wall fell, been elected mayor in the first democratic elections since the end of the Second World War and blessed the town with unparalleled economic recovery. He brought Daimler-Benz, Thyssen and Germany's leading engine manufacturer MTU to Ludwigsfelde. He created thousands of jobs and was regarded as the most successful mayor in the former East Germany—proof that East German recovery was effective, and a symbol of German unity.

He'd been retired for three years, but was no more able to stop working than his wife. Today was in fact a day off for her; the salon was closed between Christmas and New Year. It was one of those days at the end of the year when time seems to stand still. But Brigitte Scholl wasn't one for standing still; she always had to be doing something, always seeing to something, always helping somebody. In town she was known as the Lady Di of Ludwigsfelde. Her husband was 'Napoleon'. He was five foot five and liked to wear shoes with high heels.

Heinrich Scholl was still asleep when his wife got up at half past five to take her dog out, as she did every morning. Ursus was a fourteen-year-old cocker spaniel who growled at everyone since getting bitten on the ear by another dog on a walk in the cemetery last September. Brigitte Scholl fed him dog biscuits round the clock, and while she worked, Ursus was allowed to lie under the customer's chair. For his sake, Brigitte Scholl had even gone without spending Christmas with her son in Wiesbaden this year. She had wanted to spare the dog the long journey, and putting him in kennels was not an option for her. Everything revolved around Ursus. He'd even taken to sleeping in their bed lately—to her left, where her husband used to sleep.

It was still dark when Brigitte Scholl stepped outside the door, her face not made up, her hair not done, her woolly hat pulled a long way down over her face. This was the only time of day she dared go out on the street in this state. She was alone.

The air felt cold and damp, just like the days before. They hadn't had a white Christmas, and the same grey weather was forecast for New Year's Day. She walked once up Walther Rathenau Strasse and then back down again. To the left and right of her, rows of wooden houses lined the street, all alike. Dark frontages, pointy gables, little dormer windows, front gardens, flower beds, lawns, fences, garages, hedges. The wooden housing development had been built shortly before the end of the war, in 1944, the very year of Brigitte Scholl's birth. She was a war child living in a war house. In the attic, they had found notes in Cyrillic script, left there by the Soviet prisoners of war who had built the houses for the Daimler factory workers. The Daimler works in Ludwigsfelde had been the biggest and most modern aircraft-engine factory in Europe. Three-thousand-horse-power engines were built here for German fighter bombers; the assembly hangars were well concealed in the pine-woods of the Mark of Brandenburg and had direct access to Hitler's Reichsautobahn. The first engine was built in 1937; five years later, the two-hundred-soul village had become a town of five thousand inhabitants—a faceless place with no centre, no town hall and no church. Ludwigsfelde had been

intended as a field camp for Adolf Hitler and his plans of
world conquest—and it had never really recovered.

After the war, trucks were produced here. Today, Germany's biggest naturist thermal spa was in Ludwigsfelde.
The roads, pavements and cycling paths were wide; the
motorway now had six lanes. There were car showrooms,
petrol stations and roundabouts, schools, playing fields,
shopping centres, stations, car parks, tennis courts, a town
hall, an arts centre, a museum and a library. Like a Lego
model, the town was put together out of lots of little bricks.
Another house here, a restaurant here, a savings bank here,
an old folks' home here—and whenever you thought it
couldn't go on, they started on the next industrial estate. Big
signs pointed the way to the cemetery, the station, the hospital or to Prussia Park. At the crossings, people waited for
the pedestrian lights to go green even when there wasn't a
car in sight. For dog owners, there were plastic-bag dispen-
sers for the disposal of dog dirt. Everything in Ludwigsfelde
was well ordered, clean and functional. Just like the household of Brigitte and Heinrich Scholl.

The couple had moved to the wooden housing development in the seventies. Their semi-detached house was next
to a small square with a climbing frame and flower beds,
and no longer looked like a war house. Heinrich Scholl had
knocked down walls, laid tiles and put in a fireplace and a
barbecue. The windows were new, so was the roof, and the
garden was a work of art. Visitors had been known to ask
whether they should take their shoes off before walking on

the lawn. Their hedge was also much admired. So straight. But what was most important to Brigitte Scholl was that the hedge be high. It was nobody's business what she got up to—whether she was at home by herself, whether she was well or not. She was, to all intents and purposes, still the mayor's wife—an authority in the small town—and didn't even confide her problems to her best friends there. Only her son Frank*, who had moved to Wiesbaden twenty years ago, and her friend Inge Karther*, who had left Ludwigsfelde to move to Anklam in 1961, were taken into her confidence. They were also the only ones who knew that she had ordered a grave for herself at Klotz Funeral Directors a few years ago. That too was part of the mayor's wife's sense of order: certain things should be taken care of before it's too late.

Brigitte Scholl walked back to the house. It was half past six. In her husband's room under the roof, no light was on; he was obviously still asleep, which gave her the opportunity to have a shower, get dressed, clear up, prepare breakfast and make a few phone calls in peace. Unlike his wife, Heinrich Scholl liked to sleep in and stay up late. He sometimes sat in the living room until well past midnight, drinking red wine and working at some papers or other long after she had turned in. If they went to birthday parties together, it sometimes happened that she left after dinner while he stayed on. They were very different. She loved dogs; he preferred cats. He liked drinking wine; she abhorred alcohol. He would climb six-thousand-metre-high mountains; she would rather lie on a beach on the Baltic—but most of all, she preferred to stay at home.

You wondered how the two of them had put up with one another for so long—but then you wondered that about plenty of couples who had been married as long as the Scholls and whose marriage had come to resemble a business arrangement rather than a loving relationship. It was part of the Scholls' arrangement to have breakfast together, discuss the day ahead and share out the chores. After that, they went their own ways until they eventually met at home again.

Today, on that Thursday in December, things were no different. Heinrich Scholl got up, drank his coffee, read the paper. His nine-o'clock appointment had been cancelled and the next one—lunch with an old business friend in Berlin— wasn't until one. So he had time to do a bit of shopping for his wife, go to the bank and fill up the car before checking up on the thermal spa.

The spa had been his last big project as mayor—a twenty-million-euro building that had nearly cost him his head. Too big, too expensive—and naturist into the bargain. A luxury nudist spa in working-class Ludwigsfelde—even Heinrich Scholl's friends feared that he'd taken leave of his senses. But they had been wrong. The spa was buzzing; the operating company even had plans to expand. It was a late triumph for the former mayor, which was why he was keen not to lose touch with his pet project and to help with the extension plans. Just like his wife, Heinrich Scholl needed a purpose in life. In this respect they understood each other splendidly.

Today, Brigitte Scholl intended to tidy up the house and the basement party room for the New Year's Eve celebrations. On her wedding anniversary the day before, she had had a facial and pedicure, wanting to treat herself for once, but also, as anyone who knew her could have told you, with an ulterior motive: she had wanted to scout out the competition. Her beauty salon was still doing well, in spite of the thermal spa and in spite of those other salons in and around town, which called themselves 'beauty farms' and 'health farms', and which she secretly scorned, because beauticians nowadays weren't properly trained and sold cheap products at ridiculous prices. Luckily her regular customers knew her worth, but Brigitte Scholl realised that it would soon be time to start winding down a bit and eventually to retire. The standing was hard for her, and her hands ached from the neck and face massages that were part of her standard treatment. She had already cut back her working hours to three mornings a week, and before she stopped altogether, she had to find a salon that she could recommend to her customers with a clear conscience. That much she owed them.

As expected, the facial hadn't met her demands. Her skin had shone like lard and the prices had been much higher than in her own salon. This had annoyed her, but at the same time it had also pleased her; it meant a lot to her to know that she was irreplaceable.

Ursus the dog was next on her agenda. At twelve o'clock

she would put him in the car and take him to the woods for a walk. She did this every day, whatever the weather; you could set your clock by her. Her husband had often warned her that it wasn't without risk for a woman to walk about in the woods like that by herself, especially as she didn't even have a mobile—but she only ever laughed at him. Brigitte Scholl was not afraid. She was almost seventy—who would want to hurt her?

Today her walk would take a little longer than usual, because she planned to gather some fresh moss for her flower arrangements. It was her hobby. Her entire terrace was adorned with little works of art made out of mosses, twigs, pinecones and dried berries. And not just her own terrace—she gave her moss arrangements to friends and relations, neighbours and acquaintances. Today she was going to smarten up the window boxes of an old schoolmate, Maria Zucker*. Now that Maria's husband was dying, she no longer had the time to see to these things herself; it was up to Brigitte Scholl to step in.

'You've still got Easter bunnies sitting in your window boxes,' she'd exclaimed when she'd been to see Maria a few days ago and noticed that the old, dried-up spring flower arrangements were still standing about everywhere. Maria didn't care what her flower pots looked like, but she didn't say anything. She had known Gitti—as everyone called Brigitte—for sixty years and knew that once she'd set her mind on something, there was no stopping her.

In the morning the two women spoke on the phone.

Brigitte Scholl sounded her usual self—bright, determined, energetic. She said she'd drop in with the moss in the afternoon. Another friend whom Gitti rang that morning to recommend a drug for joint pain didn't notice anything out of the ordinary either. Brigitte Scholl always knew the latest drugs on the market and the best doctors and liked to recommend them to her friends. Outside the house she had a bit of a chat with a neighbour who was taking down his Christmas decorations, and she set off for the woods a little before midday. Another neighbour saw her drive off and then come back and run into the house as if she'd forgotten something. The next time her car was sighted was near the thermal spa. Everyone in town knew Brigitte Scholl's silver Mercedes with the registration number TF-BS 700. TF stood for the district, Teltow-Fläming; BS for Brigitte Scholl. A woman who had just left the photo shop drove behind her for a short while.

At about midday, Brigitte Scholl came to Siethener Strasse, at the edge of town, and parked her Mercedes. She got out, changed into her walking shoes, put the dog on the lead and walked deep into the woods to gather moss. Her footprints petered out among the tall pine trees. Later in the day, it was only her car that was seen, being driven back into town.

Sitting at the wheel was a man.

HEINRICH SCHOLL LOOKS FOR HIS WIFE

Heinrich Scholl was kept at the thermal spa longer than planned. It was packed. The queue of waiting spa guests wound its way all through the foyer. He had arrived at lunch in Berlin over an hour late and been correspondingly late back in Ludwigsfelde. He and his wife had been going to have coffee together at 4 pm. At 4.15, he parked his car, a Nissan, in front of the house. His wife's Mercedes wasn't outside the door; there was no note on the kitchen table. She wasn't there.

He asked neighbours whether they knew where she was; he rang her friends. Nobody knew anything, but nobody was seriously worried. And so he drove on to his favourite haunt, Da Toni's, on Potsdamer Strasse. It was on the ground floor of a modern five-storey block that he had inaugurated in the nineties during his time as mayor. Opposite was the shopping centre, also built in his time, and only a few metres further on, you found yourself underneath the three-hundred-and-fifty-metre motorway bridge, where he had shown Prince Charles around a few years before. Traces of his mayoral legacy were in evidence all over town.

Heinrich Scholl was still proud of them and liked to invite friends and acquaintances on tours of the town, often ending up with a glass of red wine here in Da Toni's.

He greeted the landlord and sat down in his usual place next to the bar. It was afternoon; the restaurant was nearly empty. Heinrich Scholl ordered red wine and asked the landlord for a cigarette. He wasn't actually a smoker; he was a sportsman—a gymnast, a footballer, a rower, a mountaineer. He had climbed Kilimanjaro and Mont Blanc. But he sometimes made an exception. When his wife wasn't around.

Her life followed a clear rhythm and rigid rules. She decided how they celebrated Christmas, who came for New Year's Eve, when the leaves were raked and the hedge trimmed, how many glasses of wine her husband was allowed and when it was time to go home. When Heinrich Scholl was mayor, she had rung him up in the middle of important meetings with lists of chores, and even now that he was retired, she kept him on his toes. It was always: 'Heiner fetch this, Heiner bring that.' He did the shopping, took her car to the garage, mowed the lawn, greeted her customers. When her friend Inge rang from Anklam, his wife would call him to the phone so he could say hello to her. Like a child. Two days ago, when her school friend Maria had dropped in, Brigitte Scholl had made her husband interrupt his morning's newspaper reading and recite a poem about a candle for Maria.

And so Scholl relished his moments of peace and freedom in Da Toni's all the more. Here, the landlord took his coat and asked: 'A glass of red wine as usual, Herr Bürger-meister?' Here, he was held in respect.

Heinrich Scholl stayed about an hour, talking to the landlord, who was in fact from Macedonia, but had, Scholl thought, mastered the finer points of Italian cuisine. They discussed the possibility of a terrace, and a conservatory for smokers. At about six o'clock, Heinrich Scholl paid and got back in his car.

By now it was dark outside. The day guests from the thermal spa were returning to their living rooms. Television sets flickered in the windows. It was the time of year when they showed old fairy-tale films. The roads seemed even quieter than usual. Now and then there was a bang from an early New Year's Eve rocket. In Heinrich Scholl's house there was still no light on; his wife's car was neither out the front nor in the garage. Scholl set off to look for her again, this time in earnest. He rang at the neighbours' doors, drove round to the house of the friend his wife had been going to gather moss for, and asked an acquaintance, who had been a detective superintendent until retirement, whether it was too early to involve the police. The superintendent said that the best thing to do was to ask whether there had been an accident anywhere and whether Gitti wasn't perhaps in hos-pital. He offered to ring some of his old police colleagues, but then couldn't get hold of anyone.

At about eight o'clock, Heinrich Scholl showed up at the town police station, a shack only a few metres from the motorway and not exactly one of Ludwigsfelde's showpieces.

The policeman on duty was a young man with glasses and a goatee who did not recognise Heinrich Scholl. Scholl had to begin by pointing out to him that he'd been mayor until three years ago. The young officer didn't take his concerns about his wife particularly seriously either. You don't report a person missing after three or four hours, he said. 'Your wife is a free citizen in a free country and she can do what she wants.' Maybe she was at a friend's house, or with a man. What kind of a relationship did the couple have then?

The young policeman did, however, inform his supervisor, and *he* knew Scholl. He had the town searched for Brigitte Scholl, checked her wardrobe to see if anything was missing, looked to see if her toothbrush was there. Back at the police station, he issued a missing person report: 'Missing: Brigitte Scholl, née Knorrek, 67 years old, 165 cm, slightly stocky, dark blond hair, pierced ears, wearing an all-weather jacket and boots. Accompanying objects: silver Mercedes, registration TF-BS 700, and greyish brown cocker spaniel with harness'.

A few hours later, shortly before midnight, a helicopter circled the woods with a thermal-imaging camera. Accustomed to the steady drone of the motorway, the people of Ludwigsfelde wondered whether something had happened—perhaps a road accident.

Heinrich Scholl walked around among the trees with a torch. It was the middle of the night; the woods were dark and deep. The retired superintendent, who was also troubled by the events, saw Heinrich Scholl and invited him to patrol the roads with him—not a trace of the car. The superintendent gave Heinrich Scholl a lift home and kept him company for a little while. Heinrich Scholl drank red wine and more red wine, and he smoked again. At about half past two, he fell asleep.

Three hours later he was woken by the ringing of his phone. His son wanted to know whether his mother had turned up, and announced that he was setting off for Ludwigsfelde. Heinrich Scholl lay down again and tried to get some more sleep. It was just gone six, the time when Brigitte Scholl usually got back from her morning walk with Ursus. All was quiet in the house.

The morning passed with phone calls and visits. Another policeman came by and questioned Heinrich Scholl about his wife's habits—what she did, where she spent her weekends. Scholl told him about her son and her friends—and how she liked to go to the Bleiche at the weekends, a health farm in the Spree Woods, but that she'd hardly been lately, because of the dog. The policeman suggested cancelling her debit card and ringing the Bleiche. A patrol car drove through the forest area and the town centre.

Heinrich Scholl asked the vet Werner Singer*, a friend of the family, to help him look for Gitti. Singer was a huntsman; he knew the woods. He wanted to set off immediately, but Heinrich Scholl preferred to wait for his son, Frank. At about two, the three of them drove to the woods in the vet's pick-up truck, past the cemetery entrance and along the main road towards Siethen, stopping just short of the asparagus field—exactly the same way Brigitte Scholl had driven the day before. By now, more than twenty-four hours had passed; the sky was as grey as the day before, the air damp. The men wore sturdy footwear and all-weather jackets. They searched on both sides of the forest path for clues, for some kind of sign; they called her name. Gitti. Brigitte. Mum.

No reply. Nothing.

They searched for an hour. Vet and son were ready to turn back, but Heinrich Scholl wanted to keep going until darkness fell, and suggested looking in another part of the woods where Brigitte Scholl also liked to walk. They had just set off when Frank stopped in his tracks as if struck by lightning and stared at the forest floor, where two shoes, two black women's shoes, stood neatly one beside the other, like on the shelf in his parents' hall.

'There's something here,' he called. 'There are shoes here.' Heinrich Scholl and the vet approached. The three of them stared at the shoes. The vet explored the surrounding area and discovered, not far away, two mossy mounds. One was small and round, the other bigger and longer. Peeping out of the big one were two feet; out of the smaller one, copper-coloured fur.

The ambulance was first on the scene; then came the police and forensics. Heinrich Scholl had to vomit and asked for a tranquilliser. An extensive area was cordoned off; forensics got to work; the police began their inquiries. There was no longer any doubt—and soon half the town would know. Brigitte Scholl, the former mayor's wife, was dead, murdered on a walk in the woods in broad daylight.

A sex murder, people thought. A compulsive offender going the rounds. For days, policemen searched the woods and flew over Ludwigsfelde in helicopters. Parents wouldn't let their children out of the house by themselves, joggers changed their routes, rumours circulated about Eastern European gangs, the Russian mafia and robber-murderers. Every suspicious car, every unfamiliar person was reported. The New Year's Eve fireworks seemed a little quieter this year.

Heinrich Scholl appeared spaced out, as if stunned. His son stayed with him for the first days; they discussed the most important things. On 31 December there was a ring at the door. Friends of the Scholls had come to the New Year's Eve party with sparkling wine and doughnuts. Brigitte Scholl had invited them a week before, when everything was still all right. They hadn't heard anything; they stood on the doorstep like visitors from another age. Heinrich Scholl said: 'Gitti's dead and the dog too.' He couldn't say any more, he told them; the police were still investigating. A few days later, a death notice appeared in the local newspaper, expressing, in effect, Scholl's wish to be left alone by the public. 'In silent mourning. Closest family and friends only to attend the urn burial.'

That Brigitte Scholl had made preparations for her funeral while she was still alive came as a surprise to Heinrich Scholl; his wife hadn't mentioned it to him. She wanted a modest urn burial and a plain gravestone with her name on it. Only her closest friends and relations were to attend; Frank was to give the eulogy. The deceased woman's instructions were cautiously conveyed to Heinrich Scholl by Herr Klotz, the funeral director from across the road. It was a final message from his wife and it was not a message of love. Brigitte Scholl had insisted on having the grave to herself, even after his death. For forty-seven years they had shared a table and a bed; in the end, she cast him out.

The funeral was small and oppressive. It was over three weeks since they had found Brigitte Scholl in the woods and it still wasn't clear what had happened or why. The police didn't seem to be getting anywhere with their investigations; the rumours were getting wilder and wilder. There was talk of a mutilated corpse, of the Thai mafia, of Polish gangs and political conspiracies. While her friends and family stood here in the cemetery, the murderer was at large.

Frank spoke a few tearful words. Heinrich Scholl was pale and silent; his wreath was the largest. On the bow it said: 'Lovingly, your Heiner.'

Two days later—the flowers were still fresh—a task force drew up outside the wooden house in Rathenau Strasse. When Heinrich Scholl opened the door, he saw local policemen who played on his football team—also plain clothes police and men in white protective suits, who had been instructed to search his house. The public prosecutor handed him a warrant for his arrest: he was under strong suspicion of the heinous murder of his wife. Heinrich Scholl was able to pack his tablets and his identity card. Then he was led away.

FIFTY YEARS EARLIER—
A YOUTH IN LU

Brigitte Knorrek was the most beautiful woman in town. Not a classical beauty: her legs were a little too short for that, her nose a little too long and her hips a little too heavy. It was more that Brigitte Knorrek was striking. She shone. No one else had such perfectly waved hair, such a red pout, such skilfully plucked eyebrows and such an impressive décolleté. What was more, she knew it. She walked the streets of Ludwigsfelde like a model on a catwalk.

Those who saw her still rave today about the girl in the stiffened petticoat who walked across the fairground with swaying hips and treated her schoolmates to candy floss and dodgem-car rides. The girls got the candy floss and the boys got to ride in her dodgem car; one after the other, they climbed in with her and then out again. If she took a special shine to one of them, he got to stay in for another round. Brigitte Knorrek was a kind of jackpot.

The mothers of Ludwigsfelde warned their sons about the girl, but of course that only spurred them on. Brigitte Knorrek was not only attractive; she also had a reputation for being rich and generous. Her parents were from Gleiwitz in Upper Silesia. They had had to leave their big hair salon and their house when they fled west from the Russians. They had wanted to go to Berlin, but only got as far as Ludwigsfelde—Lu, as people called it—a town set amid Brandenburg's pinewoods, with nothing but a station, a bar and the ruins of the munitions factory.

People wore trousers sewn from horse blankets, exchanged their valuables for turnips and potatoes with the farmers from the neighbouring villages and made soup out of dandelions and stinging nettles. But Brigitte Knorrek's parents were soon as well off as in Gleiwitz. Not long after their arrival, they opened the first hair salon in Ludwigsfelde since the war. It was in a small residential street between the station and the motorway. People always need a haircut.

Everyone went to the Knorreks; everyone knew the classy mother, the hunchbacked father, the severe aunt, the sprightly grandma, the beautiful Brigitte and her sister, Ursula, who had found work with a big American cosmetics company in West Berlin. The Knorreks were the first to be able to afford a car, wore clothes of good material, and when Brigitte Knorrek came home from school, there was always a big tureen of soup waiting on the table.

She seldom came home alone; she almost always brought hungry children with her. Dieter, a boy from a neighbouring village, would wait at the Knorreks' in Theaterstrasse until his mother, a nurse, came to pick him up. Inge, a pale, sickly girl, came for lunch every day and was rigged out by her friend like a dressing-up doll. 'Come on, Inge,' she would shout. 'Let's try on some new outfits and go to West Berlin. See if anything fits you.' And she would throw all her clothes on the bed, preparing for their trip. Then there was Heiner, a taciturn boy two classes above Brigitte Knorrek. He had it hardest of all.

Heinrich Scholl lived on the other side of the motorway in a small house with a big garden. The garden was lovely; there was an apple tree and a cherry tree which the grown-ups sat under on warm summer evenings, drinking schnapps and playing cards with the neighbours. You could have had a wonderful time there, climbing trees and running around, but in Heinrich Scholl's childhood there was no question of that. He was only allowed in the garden to prune the roses or mow the lawn. If he was disobedient, his father took the hoe and clouted him over the back with it. His mother hit him with the chopping board.

Heiner was unloved from birth. He was born in those winter days of 1943 when Hitler's army was defeated at Stalingrad, the air raids began on German towns and the allied forces dropped the first bombs on the Ludwigsfelde munitions factory, where Heinrich Scholl's father, Erich, was among the workers. His mother, Elfriede, was forty-three years old. For a long time, Elfriede Scholl had hoped for a child of her own, and when it hadn't worked out, she had adopted a girl from the home. The girl was called Christa; when Heinrich Scholl was born she was ten years old and it was hard enough to feed her. There was no room for another child in his mother's life, not any more.

Before the war, Elfriede Scholl had been a cashier at the cheese counter in the Berlin department store Kaufhaus des Westens, and worn fur coats and hats like the customers she sold cheese to. Her husband had worked as a lathe oper- ator at Daimler in Berlin. They had had a good life until he was moved to the aircraft-engine works in Ludwigsfelde in 1936. They may have had a new house with a garden, but the town was a dump, and the big factory, their only reason for moving there, lay in ruins nine years after their arrival. Erich Scholl no longer had work and they had to share the house with his sister-in-law's family, who had fled from Silesia. There were nine of them living in one downstairs room, a kitchen and two little garret rooms.

In 1948, Heinrich Scholl's father finally found work in a uranium mine in the Ore Mountains, but it was the worst work imaginable. For two years he stuck it out in the dank, lightless underground shafts. When he returned to his family in Ludwigsfelde, the big strapping man had become a coughing, boozing tyrant who bawled at his wife and beat his son.

Heinrich Scholl's earliest childhood memory is of the day he slipped in the garden of his parents' house and fell in the cesspit. He only just managed to get a handhold and crawl back onto the grass on all fours. He stank to high heaven; he felt sick. His father found him on the grass next to the pit, and perhaps it was the last time that Heinrich Scholl hoped to be comforted the way other children were when something awful happened to them. He never forgot his father's blows. When Erich Scholl died a few years later, his son didn't shed a tear.

He didn't expect anything of his parents, didn't wonder at their severity or their ignorance; he thought he was a bad boy who didn't deserve to be treated any better. When he was eight years old, his adoptive sister, Christa, gave birth to a son. She called him Gerhard, and for reasons Heinrich Scholl couldn't fathom, this new child was the object of all the love and attention that had never been bestowed on him. His mother picked little Gerhard up when he cried; she hugged and kissed him when he fell down and hurt himself. He had caught polio in kindergarten and fell down a lot; when he did, he would scream like a stuck pig and Heinrich Scholl was always the one to get the blame.

He went to school, he had to take care of the garden and the household—and now he had to take care of the sick boy too. When Gerhard was asleep at last, his mother would come home from her work in the co-op store and, without a word, she would tip onto the table the grocery coupons her customers had paid with. Heinrich Scholl had to sit up until far into the night, sticking them onto newspaper with flour paste. His friend Hans recalls how Heinrich Scholl some-times turned up outside his house. 'He didn't ring the bell; he just waited on the street until I spotted him.' When Hans wanted to pick him up to go swimming, Heinrich Scholl's mother would scream through the house: 'You're not going anywhere until the lawn's been mown.'

School was the only place where Heinrich Scholl felt

safe. The teachers were kind to him; they liked this boy who was so clever, so hardworking and conscientious. He was good enough to go on to grammar school after eighth form, but his mother wouldn't hear of it. She wanted her son to learn a trade and earn money. Heinrich Scholl was to become a panel beater. It was the first time he went against his mother's wishes. He didn't want to be a panel beater. He was short and slightly built and good at painting. The headmaster sent for his mother and told her that her son was far too clever to leave school. She said she didn't care; he had to earn money; she couldn't keep up the house by herself. The headmaster promised to help with the school fees. A hundred and fifty marks a month. She agreed to that.

In comparison with Heinrich Scholl's life, Brigitte Knorrek's was paradise. Gitti was the youngest in the family—an autumn crocus. She had her own room and was always getting beautiful clothes and West German marks from her sister in Berlin. The family flat was on the same floor as the hair salon; even in the hall it smelt of fresh soap, and when Gitti's mother saw Heinrich Scholl she would call out: 'Hello, Heiner, how are you? Are you hungry?'

Frau Knorrek was a tall woman with severe features, who had to run the show alone, because her husband, the master barber, may have been small and old and hunchbacked, but he still liked chasing after other women and spending the salon takings in the bar. She liked the small, helpful boy; he was so different from her spoilt daughter, who took money from the shop kitty without asking and stood half the class tickets to the funfair. Heiner didn't mind helping out in the salon, washing the floor, fetching coal from the cellar. He soon came to the Knorreks' every day, and because he was always slipped a few marks for helping out and always handed the money over at home, his mother made no objection.

Besides Gitti and her mother, Gitti's grandma was also part of the household, and her aunt Anni often called in too. They were all strong, energetic women, who had learnt in the difficult days of the war to rely solely on themselves and not to mince matters. Gitti, who was born in September 1944, only knew about the war from her mother's meagre accounts. She had no memories at all of the salon in Gleiwitz or the flight west. Her home was the shop in Ludwigsfelde with its adjustable chairs and its hood dryers, its clean-shaven gentlemen and its permed ladies. A small, self-contained world, where she wielded the sceptre like a queen. Gitti was direct, self-assertive, uncompromising. She didn't ask if she could do a thing; she just did it, and she would brook no argument. When Heiner brought his friend Hans to lunch, she sometimes sent Hans home again, because she didn't like his shirt. Her girlfriends got told how to do their hair, and anyone who ignored her was given a hard time. One girl in Gitti's class, who paid no heed when she was advised that her bun didn't go with her side-swept fringe, was 'Frau Hitler' for ever afterwards.

Heinrich Scholl's best friend Hans couldn't stand Gitti's airs and graces, and stopped going to her house for lunch.

Some of the girls in her class also kept their distance, because they didn't want to be snubbed. But most of them weren't bothered by Gitti's manner. 'It's just the way she was,' her friend Inge says. 'If she said a sweater was blue, not red, then blue it was. But she didn't mean any harm by it.'

'She wasn't at all uptight; she was a real mate,' one of Brigitte Scholl's male school friends says, and tells how in tenth form they went to their chemistry teacher's house together to get him to give them their exam questions. 'And who came up with the idea? Who was right up there at the front? Brigitte!' He has forgotten how it turned out, he says, but he still clearly remembers her fearlessness.

The salon became Heinrich Scholl's home from home. He felt at ease among the strong women who thanked him for his help, always had a dish of soup for him and even looked after him when he was ill. His stomach often hurt and Gitti's mother would give him 'rolling cures'. She made him a pot of camomile tea, swaddled him in hot towels and turned him from his belly onto his back and back again until he felt better.

He was still Gitti's school friend, the poor boy from the terrible home, but after the death of the hunchbacked Herr Knorrek, Heinrich Scholl slipped imperceptibly into the role of the man in the house. Gitti's mother left more and more of the handiwork to him and even asked his advice on her salon. Heinrich Scholl was hardworking, clever and as uncomplicated as a trusty servant. It just wasn't quite clear to anyone what the relationship was between the trusty servant and the daughter of the house; they probably weren't so sure themselves.

He helped her with her maths homework. She showed him how to embroider little mats and knit a scarf. In the summer they cycled to the gravel pit to swim or sunbathed on the deserted motorway. When Brigitte Knorrek had an admirer to visit, she would vanish into her room with him, while Heinrich Scholl sat outside the door with her friend Inge and played a round of Ludo. Or two. Until Gitti and her admirer re-emerged.

'Gitti and Heiner were like children together; it wasn't a proper relationship,' says Dieter Fahle, the boy from the neighbouring village. 'Heiner always just tagged along with the Knorreks. He came from an awful home. Nowadays you'd say he was damaged by his environment.'

Brigitte Scholl's friend Inge says: 'They always got on well, did Heiner and Brigitte. But Heiner wasn't an option for most of the girls, because he was so short.'

Heinrich Scholl says: 'Gitti's boyfriends were in a different league from me. But sometimes I was allowed to help out sexually. I may have been short, but I was a good gymnast and the only one of her men who managed to climb secretly into her room from the courtyard.'

Gitti had several boyfriends. One was called Wolfgang and waited for her at the station in Teltow every evening. He was apprenticed to an electrician there; she helped out in a beauty salon. Wolfgang cycled from Ludwigsfelde to Teltow and took the train back just so he could travel with Gitti.

The train—an old one with a steam engine and wooden seats—left at 7 pm on the dot. At 7.20 it arrived in Ludwigsfelde. They only had twenty minutes, but they had those twenty minutes all to themselves, because the shift workers took an earlier train. When they arrived in Ludwigsfelde, they straightened their clothes, then Gitti sat on the crossbar of Wolfgang's bike and got a lift home to Theaterstrasse.

Manfred Schlögel, who was always known as Schnuppi, met Gitti at Lake Siethen. He was three years older than her, a big broad-shouldered fellow. When he shot down Potsdamer Strasse on his Java 350, people turned to look— all the more when Gitti was riding pillion in a short skirt. Schnuppi belonged to the same rowing club as Heinrich Scholl and his friends. They would all sit in one boat: in the middle, the powerful Schnuppi had to keep the pace up, while little Heiner, as the stroke, had to set the rhythm.

Gitti sat on a rug on the bank and looked on.

When the day drew to a close and the men got out of the boat, there was drinking and merrymaking, and whoever wanted to be alone got Gitti's school friend Maria to give them the keys to her mother's bungalow on the neighbouring plot. Sometimes Maria's mother turned up unexpectedly, and Gitti and Schnuppi had to jump quickly into the lake and swim back to the boathouse.

Beside the motorbike, Schnuppi owned a canoe. It had a cover that protected its occupants from the weather and hid them from view. This made for a safer meeting place than the bungalow, but summer was soon over and in the winter there was only Gitti's little room next to the salon, where her mother could burst in at any moment. One evening, Gitti told Schnuppi she had something to tell him: she was seeing Ulli, the dentist's son.

'She gave me the brush-off, completely out of the blue,' says Manfred Schlögel. 'There was no reason whatsoever. But that's just the way she was; my mother had warned me.'

THE SUMMER OF '61

The next summer came: the summer of 1961. Ludwigsfelde now boasted a clubhouse and wedding-cake-style houses like the ones on Berlin's Stalinallee. The ruins of the old Daimler works were cleared away and a new works was opened where they built twenty-cylinder engines, East Germany's first jet plane and a motor scooter called the 'Weasel'. Half the town worked there.

Schnuppi was a lathe operator in Hall 8. Heinrich Scholl was apprenticed to a toolmaker along with Assi, as he called his friend Hans. Women were in demand too, but factory work wasn't Gitti's thing. She wanted to become a beautician and persuaded her friend Inge to join her. The only institute that trained beauticians was in Dresden and it cost three thousand marks to train there.

Frau Knorrek paid for Gitti without demur, but Inge's parents couldn't afford the expensive college. The young women went their separate ways.

It was to be a summer of separations. But none of them knew that yet. For now, the days were long and hot and full of promise. The boys from Lake Siethen had finished school and decided to meet up in Bansin, on the Baltic Sea, home to the biggest campsite in East Germany. The girls stayed in Ludwigsfelde. Gitti had been given a dog by her new boy-friend—a small brown cocker spaniel. And camping wasn't her thing anyway.

Heiner and Assi took the suburban train to Oranienburg at the end of the line and from there they cycled all the way up the B96. They reached Bansin in the middle of the night. They had earned fifty marks from a farmer, sent a sailor's kitbag packed with tinned food and a spirit cooker on ahead by post and devised an ingenious system for surviving the next three weeks. They collected whatever departing holidaymakers left behind—sun-tan oil, bottles of beer, tins of food. And they cadged food off the girls who worked in the hotel kitchens—bread, cheese, sausage, ham and any-thing else left over from the cold buffets. It worked well. They had plenty to eat, swam in the Baltic and flirted with the kitchen girls. Heinrich Scholl and his friend remember every day in Bansin as hot and sunny.

Schnuppi, Gitti's former love, arrived in Bansin on his motorbike a few days after Heinrich Scholl. It was 30 July 1961; he still remembers the exact date. In the evening, he headed for the beer tent. Hundreds of young people were sit-ting inside at long tables. Schnuppi sat down with two boys who were playing the guitar. '"Tutti Frutti" and all that,' he says. 'All the great music from the West.'

The guitarists were attracting more and more beer-tent visitors, including a group of young men with shorn heads.

Schnuppi knew the 'baldies' from the beach. One was a barber's apprentice and had given his mates a 'holiday cut'. Manfred Schlögel—Schnuppi—says they were actually perfectly harmless.

The boys with the shorn heads began to dance, in between the benches and on the tables. 'Off the tables,' the landlord yelled. The baldies laughed and carried on dancing. The landlord fetched the local policeman; the local policeman fetched a riot squad. The baldies suddenly sprouted hats and vanished into the crowd, but one of them was caught and led off. 'Let him go,' Schnuppi and his friends shouted. The police got out their batons. 'Workers hitting workers!' Schnuppi yelled. Each sentence, he says, was to cost him a year.

He was thrown onto a truck, taken to a cell in Heringsdorf and released again the next morning. He was told to report to the campsite guard a few days later and show his ID. When he did so, he was arrested again. Manfred Schlögel had no idea what lay in store for him. 'I was so naïve. I told the guard he should ask his boss to get a move on, because I didn't have much holiday left. And that I was in the B-pool of the national rowing team and had to compete for the Blue Ribbon of Warnow in the championships. I'll never forget the look he gave me.'

For four days and nights, from 9 August until 13 August 1961, Manfred Schlögel was interrogated in Rostock. The 13th was a Sunday—that, too, he remembers. 'On the Monday, the interrogator danced about like Rumpelstiltskin and said: "None of you are going back to Berlin. We're building a wall for undesirable elements like you.'"

Heinrich Scholl and his friend Hans were unaware of their friend's troubles—the campsite was big and the beer tent too expensive for them. They were busy with their little day-to-day struggles for survival, went swimming and met the girls from the kitchen in the evenings, and had no idea what had happened to Schnuppi. Nor did they know that the borders had just been closed. In the middle of Berlin a wall was put up overnight.

Until then people had still been able to go back and forth between East and West Berlin. Many worked in West Berlin, where they were paid in the more valuable deutsch-mark, and lived in East Berlin, where rents were lower. They would go to the movies in the West and grocery shopping in the East. But on 13 August, traffic between the two parts of the city stopped dead. Families were ripped apart and jobs lost. A country was divided, a new era begun.

Manfred Schlögel was sentenced to five and a half years in prison in Bautzen 'for subversive acts and gang formation'. Brigitte Knorrek was the only one who sent him parcels. They were filled with ham, sausage and jam—only food was allowed. When Manfred Schlögel returned to Ludwigs-felde on his release, she was married and had a son.

WEDDING

It is hard to say just how Brigitte Knorrek and Heinrich Scholl came to be a couple. Only one thing's for certain: it's not a particularly romantic story.

Gitti was only twenty when they married. The carefree times—when her friends had dropped in and out and she had gone to the cinema on Potsdamer Platz with Inge or careered through the streets on Schnuppi's Java—were long gone by then. A wall had been built around West Berlin. Inge had married and moved away to a town in the north. Schnuppi was in jail. And in May of that year, 1964, Brigitte Knorrek had given birth to a son.

The father was a tall, good-looking man from nearby Kleinmachnow—Gitti's type. She had met him dancing and he visited her a few times, but was soon interested in another girl. Frau Knorrek, who was Catholic and feared for her reputation in town, was frantic. There was only one way to limit the damage: her daughter must get married. This is where good old Heinrich came into play. He was now twenty-two, had completed his apprenticeship as a toolmaker and was studying at the school of engineering in

Riesa, an industrial town on the Elbe. But he was still under his mother's thumb. She grumbled that he would drive them all to ruin and demanded that he spend every free minute working and earning money.

The best-paid work was doing night shifts at the pit furnace in the Riesa steelworks. Fifty marks he got for eight hours at the furnace, pulling out red-hot moulds and knocking them off. From the works, he'd walk straight to the station without any sleep and take the train to Ludwigsfelde, where his next chores were waiting. He helped Frau Knorrek in the salon, lugged coal for the neighbours and, if he had any time to spare in the evenings, he would paint landscapes in oils, which he copied from postcards to sell to people in town. In the summer vacation he worked as an extra in Gojko Mitić films. The Serbian actor was famous in East Germany for his westerns, in which the Native Americans, not the white settlers, were the heroes. Heinrich played a Native American, donning a special costume for the part. Every pfennig he earned was handed over to his mother. She never said thank you.

One weekend, when he had just got back from a night shift at the furnace, she announced to him that she was going to sell the house and move to West Berlin with little Gerhard. The child's mother, Christa, had met an American and wanted to emigrate to Oklahoma with him. Everything was planned. Elfriede Scholl, who had just retired, had applied for an exit visa; the house was to go to an uncle; Heinrich Scholl was to keep the little room under the roof.

He wasn't asked for his opinion.

Heinrich didn't know what to say. It wasn't news to him that his mother didn't love him; he was just surprised that she could live without him. 'Everything I'd done up until then had only one purpose: to earn money for her. Without me and my extra earnings, she wouldn't be able to manage.'

Elfriede Scholl simply vanished from his life, without big goodbye scenes, without tears. He now had no father, no mother and no home. When he came back to Ludwigsfelde from Riesa at the weekend, he climbed up to the garret room in his parents' house like a stranger. Six square metres were all that remained to him. He wasn't allowed to enter the other rooms or go in the garden.

At the weekends he often stayed in Riesa now, spending the money from the night shifts at the steelworks in the harbour pub or at a dance in Merzdorf. The students were not especially popular with the locals, but they were popular with the girls—particularly Heinrich Scholl. He was the best dancer. Twist and boogie and rock 'n' roll—he could do everything, swivelling his hips like Elvis Presley, and throwing the girls in the air and catching them again.

There was one girl he danced with a lot. Her father worked in the steelworks; she worked in the cotton spinning mill. Heinrich Scholl sometimes went home with her after the dance. She became pregnant at almost exactly the same time as Brigitte Knorrek and, like her, gave birth to a son.

A week after the birth, Heinrich Scholl left his son's mother. He has never seen his son; he doesn't even know his name, he says. The girl understood. 'We came to a very sensible agreement. The welfare office stipulated how much alimony I had to pay. I had it transferred every month until his eighteenth birthday.' They simply weren't a good match. Her parents were very uncouth, he says; they both drank. It reminded him of his own home—of the life he was trying to escape.

One of Brigitte Scholl's friends says that in fact the girl went to the head of the engineering school and complained that she had been deserted by her child's father. The school put pressure on Heinrich Scholl to marry the girl, and because he didn't want that, he quickly married Gitti instead.

His best friend Hans only knows that everything went very fast. 'Heiner came to me just before the Christmas holidays and said: "I'm with Brigitte now. We're going to get married."' His reaction had been: 'You can't do that; you know what she's like.' Hans Streck wouldn't have put up with Gitti for a single day and didn't understand why his clever friend was marrying a woman who was nothing but a younger version of his mother. But these objections seemed not to get through to Heinrich Scholl. His friend says that Heiner was probably looking for a home—that he wanted a family. 'He had no one left. His father was dead; his mother was in the West; his uncle was horrid to him.'

Brigitte Scholl's friend Inge says that everything happened at once. 'She was pregnant. Then Frank's father walked out on her, or she walked out on him; I don't rightly know. In any case she was pleased when Heiner took her. She had Frank to think of and he was in good hands with Heiner.'

Heinrich Scholl says that he had hinted to her when she was pregnant that he was at her disposal, and then a few weeks later she had asked him and he had said yes. 'We knew each other. We knew what we were like. She could depend on me entirely. She needed a father for Frank. It was the most convenient arrangement.'

Did he love Gitti?

'I don't know,' he says. 'I certainly liked her a lot, but we never told each other that. It's not the way we were. We didn't need that.'

Brigitte Knorrek and Heinrich Scholl's wedding took place on 28 December 1964. There was no lavish party, no guest list, no carriage, no white dress. Few people even knew about it.

The date was decided for them: in 1964, for the first time since the Wall had been built, there were to be passes available between Christmas and New Year's Eve permitting West Berliners to cross to East Berlin for a few hours—and Heinrich Scholl wanted his mother to be there. He hadn't seen her since she had left Ludwigsfelde and he hoped she would be proud of him, now that he had conquered Brigitte Knorrek, the hairdressers' daughter.

On the morning of 28 December, they took the train to East Berlin. They had left the baby with Brigitte Knorrek's mother in Ludwigsfelde. It was a cold day. She wore a dark jacket and skirt, he a suit. At Friedrichstrasse Station—the border crossing point known as the 'Palace of Tears', the site of many emotional reunions and farewells—they met Heinrich Scholl's mother. She had brought little Gerhard with her, now a teenager. They stood facing one another in divided Berlin, surrounded by border soldiers and flustered people with bags and suitcases. A mother, her son, his young bride. It was the moment Heinrich Scholl had been waiting for. He had thought something might happen—that the knot might loosen.

'They came out of the Palace of Tears,' he says, 'Gerhard and this little mother in her coat and her fur collar. I hugged and kissed them. But there was no response from her. She simply didn't like me. I resigned myself to it then. What did I care?'

The marriage ceremony took place in the registry office at Alexanderplatz. There was a picture of Walter Ulbricht, the East German leader, hanging on the wall, and the registrar reeled off something about the importance of the socialist family in socialist society. They said 'Yes', exchanged rings, kissed. Then, in their thin coats, they walked down Stalinallee to Café Moskau. Café Moskau was East Berlin's most modern restaurant. The dining room was bright and empty, the prices steep, the waiter unfriendly. He took their order, brought food and drinks, and they had soon had plenty to eat. But they couldn't leave. The pass was valid for the entire day, but they had nowhere else to go.

'It was awful,' Heinrich Scholl says. 'The waiter kept

coming to our table and asking if we wanted anything else. We had to sit on our hands all day and couldn't go out. It was much too cold for that.' When evening came at last, they took his mother and Gerhard back to Friedrichstrasse Station and returned to Ludwigsfelde. Heinrich Scholl did not go back to the room at his uncle's that evening. He slept with Gitti in her childhood bedroom, her little boy in the room next door.

He had a home.

THE DARE

When Heinrich Scholl returned to Riesa after the Christmas vacation, it was with a ring on his finger. Otherwise nothing had changed. His room was in an old barracks; it had three bunk beds, three cupboards and a table in the middle. He shared it with five other men and a great quantity of vermin, including some mice they caught and kept in roll-mop jars and fed with leftovers.

Heinrich Scholl studied and at night he worked in the steelworks, but he no longer had to hand the money over to his mother; he could keep it for himself. He was a frugal person; he didn't mind sleeping in the barracks, eating sausages out of a tin or drinking beer in the smoky harbour pub with the other students of an evening.

Gitti was different. Nothing was good enough for the hairdressers' daughter with a sister in the West, and she was keen to let others know. Only once did she visit her husband in Riesa. It was a disaster, in spite of Heinrich Scholl's best efforts. He met her at the station with flowers, strolled through town with her, showed her the town hall, the Sachsenhof Hotel and the River Elbe. He wanted to offer her

something, to show her his world. Riesa may have been a
workers' town like Ludwigsfelde, but it was bigger and more
cosmopolitan. There was a harbour, where ships arrived
and unloaded, an old city centre and lots of young people,
who studied there like him. He knew his way around and
was greeted on the street, but Gitti acted the fine lady and
refused to be impressed by anything.

Her big scene came when Heinrich Scholl tried to take
her to his favourite bar, the harbour pub, with his friend
Hans. Gitti took one look at the smoky room and the men
with their beer steins, then turned on her heels and said: 'I'm
not going in that pub.'

She insisted on going to the most expensive establish-
ment in town, the Sachsenhof, and in a show of generosity,
she treated her husband and his friend to dinner. As they
were eating, she told Hans that it wasn't done to mash
your potatoes; you should just crush them slightly with your
fork, if you had to. 'Assi, you can't do that—if anyone saw
you,' she said. Hans Streck still remembers the incident fifty
years on, so odd did he find Brigitte Scholl's behaviour. But
Heinrich Scholl's reaction was odd too. He sat there and
didn't say a word.

Heinrich Scholl was different when he was with his
wife—subdued, almost cowed. This had always been the
case, even when they were still at school. But now it was more
noticeable. Maybe because Heinrich Scholl was usually very
different: self-confident, impudent, daring, someone who
didn't seem afraid of anything.

One evening, the boys from his barracks decided to go out for a beer together. Each of them was to chip in with a few marks, but Heinrich Scholl had no money and had to come up with something. A dare. He looked at the jars where they kept the mice and knew at once how he was going to come by his beer. Two crates of bock he was promised, if he'd bite the head off a mouse. They didn't think he'd have the guts. Heinrich Scholl took a mouse from one of the jars, held it tight, closed his eyes and bit.

'I'd do anything,' Heinrich Scholl says. 'I was a boy who was always having to prove himself.'

It was a side to him that people who knew him admired, but also found a little unnerving. Scholl's friend Hans Streck deliberates for a long time before making up his mind to tell another, similar story. It was shortly before they graduated. The final maths exams were nearly upon them and some students were afraid of failing and being thrown out of college. Their maths tutor—a short, fat, nasty piece of work, nicknamed Pig Cheek—had only recently expelled one of their classmates, and revelled in his power over the students. In each class, he would point to his bag and with a broad, sneering grin he would say: 'Your questions are in there.'

Heinrich Scholl's class decided to get the better of Pig Cheek. They had planned everything down to the last detail. In the break between classes, one of the students was to engage the tutor in a lengthy talk in the corridor, one was to keep a lookout, one was to take the exam paper out of the tutor's bag and one was to copy out the questions. Someone was soon found for the talk in the corridor—and for keeping a lookout and copying out the questions. But no one dared open Pig Cheek's bag and take out the exam paper. No one, that is, except Heinrich Scholl.

'He simply had no fear. He took every risk,' his friend Hans says. 'Even though he had absolutely no need to do it. Heiner was good at maths; even if he'd botched the exam, he'd have passed.'

Everything went off smoothly. Their tutor didn't notice anything. No one failed the maths exam. Heinrich Scholl passed all his other exams effortlessly too. At the end of the academic year, he packed up his things from the barracks and moved back to Ludwigsfelde, to his wife and son.

NATURISM

Their new flat was above the hair salon and Gitti's mother's flat. They had two rooms, a box room and a small kitchen. The box room was Frank's bedroom.

Frank was a year old and Brigitte and Heinrich Scholl didn't want another child. Heinrich Scholl says this was Gitti's decision. One child was enough for her. The topic had only been raised once. 'And we said to each other: "The scores are level between us. You have a child, I have a child. Why chance it again?"' He hadn't been particularly eager to have more children either. 'I think it's the woman's business.'

He says this soberly, almost with indifference, as if children were mere figures in life's grand account. It was in the same unexcitable way that he dealt with his stepson. He adopted him—and the other, biological father was blotted out from the life of the Scholl family like the girl from the spinning mill. There were no photos, no letters, no get-togethers. The deposit and withdrawal slips from the alimony payments were filed and locked away. Gitti was the mother, Heiner the father, Frank the child. A perfect family. Not even Gitti's closest friends were told who Frank's father was, and Heinrich Scholl applied himself to his new role as husband and family man with such vigour that no one dared question it.

Brigitte Scholl had chosen him from among all her men because he was hardworking, and in this respect he did not disappoint. She called the tune in the house; she told him what was to be done, and it would never have occurred to him to question his role. He had always carried out the Knorreks' instructions and worked through his mother's lists. Now it was his wife's lists: do the shopping, take the rubbish down, wash the kitchen floor. As a rule, Brigitte Scholl also added the precise time. She made lists for her husband, and as soon as her son could read, she made lists for him too. 'It was Gitti's way of sharing out the chores,' says Heinrich Scholl. 'I helped Frank in school and was on the parents' committee. She challenged him at home.'

In his mother-in-law's hair salon, his range of duties had, to be sure, considerably expanded. He still washed the floor, but he also had to attend to other, more fundamental things. Business wasn't what it had been. Frau Knorrek had started to drink. Sometimes she was out of it by lunchtime and had to withdraw to her flat. No one knew the reasons. Was she unhappy? Was she worried about the business? Was it a strain on her, running the salon all by herself? Did she miss her elder daughter, who now lived in Cologne? Was she kept awake at night by images of the war and the flight west? She never talked about her problems. She had always been strong Frau Knorrek—successful, well-off, generous

Frau Knorrek—and it was important to her that it should stay that way.

Looking back on this time, Heinrich Scholl later noted: 'Mother drinks heavily, salon does worse and worse. Mother is drunk in her flat from midday onwards, hairdressers do as they please. She's in the red. Gitti asks me to deal with it. I advise her to give up the hair salon and put in an application for a cosmetics business. She doesn't like the idea, because of what people might think.'

What people might think was as important to Brigitte Scholl as it was to her mother. Everyone knew the elegant Frau Knorrek and her salon. There was the station, the bar, the Daimler works, the dentist, the grocer's—and there was the hairdresser's in Theaterstrasse, where half the town met, where everyone talked about everyone else, and each piece of news, each divorce, each new baby, each affair was weighed in the balance. The hairdresser's salon was the small town's meeting place, and Brigitte Scholl knew how quickly you could lose your standing among the locals. She didn't want her mother to close the salon.

Heinrich Scholl didn't think this particularly sensible from an economic point of view, but once again he had an idea. He put in an application for a private business for his wife in Ludwigsfelde and set up a salon for her in her mother's shop. They now had two shops in one, and if need be, daughter could absorb mother's losses.

Brigitte Scholl was happy. She no longer had to go to Teltow every day and be bossed about by her employer;

she could receive her customers in her own studio. She created a file card for each one with name, age and skin type. Young and old women came to her in Theaterstrasse from Ludwigsfelde and the surrounding villages, and raved about her treatment. Brigitte Scholl knew all about the skin's acid mantle, about facial muscles and the harmony of body, mind and soul; she could blend rose petals, camomile and horsetail to create healing tinctures, massage foreheads and necks—and she was a good listener too. The business was soon doing better than her mother's; she was even earning more than her husband.

After his studies in Riesa, Heinrich Scholl had planned to start work as a technologist in the industrial plant in Ludwigsfelde. But aircraft construction was discontinued when the first jet plane got caught in a power line on its demonstration flight and never made it to Leipzig, where Walter Ulbricht was waiting with other guests of honour. The plant now produced trucks. There was no job for him.

He became a teacher at the plant's vocational college, teaching materials science, giving polytechnic classes and preparing young people from the juvenile detention centre for their training. He had to serve in the army too—a year and a half of basic military service with the Motorised Infantry Division in Stahnsdorf. He didn't want to, but army service was obligatory, and once again he found a way to set himself apart from the others. When his regimental commanding officer needed a gift for a Russian commander, Heinrich Scholl made a tinplate model of an armoured personnel carrier, fifty centimetres by ninety centimetres, which he mounted on a wooden panel. The Russian commander was delighted, and Heinrich Scholl had a new job. He no longer had to drive tanks; from now on he was allowed to make little model ones. To begin with, he made his model tanks in the barracks; later on, towards the end of his military service, he was even given special permission to make them at home.

When he returned from the army, there was a job in the car works. Heinrich Scholl's bosses found their new technologist hard to fathom. Like most East Germans, Scholl was under observation by officials of the Ministry for State Security, known as the Stasi, and by neighbours and colleagues working as Stasi informants. His Stasi file contains several pages extolling his ambition, his helpfulness and his expertise, but as soon as his attitude to the communist state is at issue, the tone changes: 'Heinrich Scholl has numerous West German contacts, is politically indecisive and hard to read, does not engage in group activities and is an employee of the indifferent, dilatory type, who no longer knows his place, associating in private only with doctors and other high-status figures.'

Heinrich Scholl was a showpiece engineer in a showpiece socialist factory, but he tried to block out the socialist part. He knew which compromises he had to accept and which he didn't. When he was invited to become a member of the German Socialist Unity Party and civilian paramilitary groups, he declined. When the invitations persisted, he took on the post of secretary of Free German Youth and registered with

Civil Defence. After that, he was left in peace for the time being. 'I always found a way of getting off lightly, you might say,' says Heinrich Scholl.

His wife knew no such worries. She had her private salon—her own little niche in the communist state. The only organisation she was a member of was the Free German Federation of Trade Unions, and she only joined that because it got her a holiday trip to the Baltic every few years.

In Ludwigsfelde, Brigitte Scholl surrounded herself with a small circle of women—others she preferred to keep at bay. To those who didn't know her, she could seem priggish and aloof. Her sister in Cologne sent her clothes, and West German money, too, so that she could shop in the state-run Intershop chain, which only accepted foreign currency and sold high-quality goods not usually available to East Germans. Gitti didn't have to join the department-store queues when there were jeans or Adidas trainers to be had. When the people of Ludwigsfelde flocked to the lake in droves to go swimming in the summer, Gitti walked past them with hat, picnic rug and hamper to her own bathing spot. It was a small clearing by one of the gravel pits that the farmers had excavated in the thirties for the construction of Hitler's motorways. You drove to Kleinbeuthen, a village near Ludwigsfelde, and then followed a narrow path along the shore. The clearing was across a field, between two birches. Everyone knew that Gitti met her friends here—and that they all swam in the nude. But it wouldn't have occurred to anyone to join them uninvited.

In the evenings, couples met to dance in the town's new clubhouse or in the bar called 'Sanssouci'. As a late wedding present from his mother, Heinrich Scholl had been given a pair of pointy black shoes and a suede coat with a fake fur collar. When he danced with Gitti, a circle formed around them.

THE UPPER CRUST
OF LUDWIGSFELDE

Gitti's mother was drinking more and more. She hardly showed up in the salon at all now and hadn't been able to keep the books for a long time. Sometimes her daughter would find her in the kitchen, lying on the floor.

In 1972 she had to close down the shop, and without the shop her daughter no longer had a place for her beauty treatments. Heinrich Scholl set his wife up in Frank's bedroom to be going on with and put in an application to exchange their flat and Gitti's mother's flat for a house.

A year later, they were allocated a semi-detached house in the wooden housing development, which had a reputation in Ludwigsfelde as a desirable neighbourhood. The house might have been old and in need of repair, but it had four hundred square metres of garden. Heinrich Scholl had walls pulled down and the roof retiled; he converted the cellar, had a bar and a big tiled bathroom put in, had a fireplace built, and a barbecue, and changed the layout of the garden. He designed everything and drew all the plans himself; friends and workmen helped him with the building work in the evenings and at the weekend.

The renovation took almost two years. Gitti's mother lived in a little room under the roof and only came downstairs in the mornings to go and buy her daily ration of schnapps in the shop across the road. One morning, she didn't emerge. Gitti found her in her room. Dead. Beside her bed were two empty bottles and an empty packet of tablets.

When customers asked what had happened, Brigitte Scholl said her mother had fallen down the stairs. She was concerned for her family's reputation. Her mother may have been a hapless drinker, but that was nobody's business. Gitti's friend Karin*, the local vet's wife, says she always tried to put on a show of perfection.

Hardly was the funeral over when Brigitte Scholl's perfect world was shattered all over again. She got a phone call: her sister Ursula in Cologne had died unexpectedly—a fall in the bathroom, she was told.

Ursula Knorrek was fifteen years older than Brigitte Scholl. She had run the Estée Lauder sales agency for Germany, Austria and Switzerland, and although she had no children, she had a big house and a husband who earned a decent salary. Brigitte Scholl had always envied her sister her eventful life. Ursula had been her role model, the big sister who had felt hemmed in living in Ludwigsfelde and left it for a world which Brigitte Scholl, in her tiny beauty salon, could only dream of. Ursula sent postcards to Ludwigsfelde from her trips around the world. Paris. Vienna. London. She went to fashion shows and met people you could gawk at in gossip magazines. Sometimes Ursula featured in the photos too.

At the funeral in Cologne, Brigitte Scholl found out that her sister had taken her own life with an overdose of tablets. But no one really knew why. All that was said was that she had had trouble coming to terms with her age.

It was 1979 and Brigitte Scholl was only in her mid-thirties. Though beauty and youth were her profession, and she stood in her salon five days a week, from eight until six, fighting signs of age, she hadn't yet realised that she herself was aging too. Most of her customers were older than she was and admired her smooth, unlined skin, her perfectly arched eyebrows, her full mouth. She was still a woman who could steal the limelight—but her sister's death made her realise that her youth too would one day be over.

Brigitte Scholl had a midlife crisis and took a lover. He was the son of a couple they were friends with—an actor, ten years younger than her. Her husband knew nothing of his wife's affair; he was busy doing up the house and sorting out her inheritance.

A few months after the death of Brigitte Scholl's sister, her brother-in-law also took his life. The house in Cologne had to be sold off and the antique furniture sent across the inter-German border to Ludwigsfelde. Heinrich Scholl still clearly recalls the trouble he had getting the furniture from Cologne over the border. He doesn't know what Gitti's feelings were. 'She never cried,' he says. 'Not in front of me at any rate—and I never cried in front of her. We were brought up tough.'

He didn't discover that his wife had betrayed him with

a young actor until years later, when he read his Stasi file.

Life went on. The house was finished at last; they had more room, a fireplace, a barbecue, two bathrooms and the furniture from the West. Brigitte Scholl led her guests around the rooms as if around a museum. An old grandfather clock here, the Biedermeier bureau there, a mahogany cupboard. She had inherited the entire household from Cologne. Rugs, crockery, cutlery, table cloths, lamps—and shop fittings for a complete beauty salon. The neighbours still remember the two big containers that stood in the street. Anything that didn't fit in the house was sold. There was soon a new car parked outside the Scholls' front door. The Stasi noted in their records that Heinrich Scholl moved in circles that belonged to 'the upper crust of Ludwigsfelde'.

In the car works, Heinrich Scholl was in charge of the new drop forge, a prestigious East German project overseen in person by Politburo member Günter Mittag. Scholl was an expert in the field and spoke better English than any of his colleagues; he led negotiations with Brits, Swedes and Austrians. Only travel abroad was barred to him. Time and again he applied for travel cadre status, and time and again his application was turned down. 'They kept saying the passport wasn't ready,' Heinrich Scholl says, 'and then the party secretary would go to Vienna or Stockholm in my place, although he didn't have the first clue. In the end, I realised the passport would never be ready.'

Heinrich Scholl wasn't getting anywhere. He didn't know where to channel his skills and his energy. He wasn't

the only one who had problems. His school friend Dieter
Fahle had trained as a glassblower after being thrown out
of the car works. His best friend Hans had applied for an
exit visa and moved to North Rhine Westphalia with his
family. One of his colleagues planned to escape, because
he was fed up with waiting for an exit visa. Scholl thought
that too dangerous and, with the help of a doctor friend, got
his workmate a medical certificate to speed up the process.
Their meetings to discuss this plan took place in Ludwigsfelde Woods. Heinrich Scholl couldn't bring himself to make
such a radical move. Everything he possessed in Ludwigsfelde had been laboriously built up. The house was finished
at last and Gitti's salon was doing better than ever before.
But much as he loved Ludwigsfelde, he was beginning to feel
hemmed in living in East Germany.

Scholl was constantly running up against walls, and
eventually he could take no more. At a meeting with the
factory's Swedish contracting partners, he was to confirm
a drop forge delivery to the value of several million marks.
It wasn't that they had any need of the delivery in Ludwigsfelde; it was just to give the Swedes the impression that the
East German economy was making good progress. Scholl
said it was nonsense. His superiors said it was the party line.

It wasn't Heinrich Scholl's line. Sitting in the meeting
with the Swedes, he explained the problem to them. He
thought his colleagues and the Stasi people at the table
didn't speak sufficiently good English. But it was evidently
enough. The next day, the director general summoned his

head technologist to his office, accused him of political sabotage and issued him with a reprimand. Heinrich Scholl stood up, left the room, got the secretary to give him pen and paper and wrote a letter of resignation.

He was now unemployed, but because there's no such thing as unemployment in a communist state, he was officially employed as his wife's caretaker. This didn't bother Scholl; it was what he did anyway. And for a man like him, even a caretaker's job had its challenges. He immediately began to come up with new projects for himself. He collected bits of coloured glass and made lamps with them, planned an extension for his old friend Dieter's house, designed a garden for Gitti's friend Gudrun, built a fireplace for the master butcher in the nearby town of Grossbeeren. He was earning no less money than his former colleagues in the car works.

Brigitte Scholl was nevertheless embarrassed. She didn't want to be married to a caretaker, not even her own.

When her customers walked down the hall to the beauty salon, they would see her husband sitting at breakfast. In the past, she had been able to say: 'My husband is head technologist.' Now she said: 'My husband's doing Dieter's extension.'

Heinrich Scholl felt her scornful glance as he went down to his cellar workshop, her reproachful silence at the supper table. He worked all day long, he earned money and still he felt like a failure. It was as if he'd moved back in with his mother.

He applied for work in local businesses—in Caputh, where the palace was being restored, and in the microchip factory in Teltow. 'At first they'd say yes, great, come and see us,' Heinrich Scholl says. 'But as soon as they read my personal file, I'd get a rejection.' In Heinrich Scholl's personal file, it said he was 'politically indifferent' and that he had sabotaged important deals in the car works with partners from non-socialist foreign countries. He hadn't had work now for six months. Gitti was growing more and more taciturn.

A neighbour who was an acrobat said that Berolina Circus was looking for a technical manager. Scholl rang up. The circus manager said he'd be glad to employ him, but he should send in a written application to be on the safe side. Two weeks later, a rejection came from the circus's personnel department. It was the last straw for Scholl.

He got in his Wartburg Tourist and drove to Berlin-Hoppegarten, where the circus had its winter quarters. The manager was standing at the entrance when Heinrich Scholl got out of his car. He knew nothing of the letter of rejection and told Scholl he could start the next day; his secretary would just draft the contract. The secretary shook her head—no, she couldn't; orders from above. The circus manager put an arm around Heinrich Scholl's shoulder, took him to the canteen and asked him: 'Have you got something to write on?'

Heinrich Scholl tore a page out of his diary; the circus manager drafted the contract.

Two days later they were travelling through the southern regions of East Germany along with elephants, tigers and giraffes.

AT THE CIRCUS

Berolina Circus was a collective combine—a big, heavily subsidised socialist company that employed dressage riders, acrobats, tightrope walkers, clowns and animal tamers. Heinrich Scholl was in charge of a hundred and thirty wagons and seventy employees. He had to choose a plot of land, organise transportation and arrange for the big top to be put up and taken down. Every three days, the circus moved to a different town; in big cities it stopped a week. Heinrich Scholl's work day began at seven o'clock; in the evenings, when the performance started, he knocked off and could read, go for a jog, do his shopping or have a look around town. After the show, the ping pong table was put up in the ring and he would play Chinese table tennis with acrobats and animal tamers until the early hours of the morning. 'We had the Leuzingers with us—the Swiss tamer family,' he says. 'Seven tigers. And Frau Böttcher with her polar bears. It was marvellous. Terrific. Like a blood transfusion.'

But the best thing about the circus was Scholl's circus caravan—three metres by seven, complete with loo, wash basin, sofa bed, table and three chairs. It was only a simple wooden box on wheels with screwed-down furniture, small windows and cheap crockery, but it was his own world.

Scholl wanted for nothing.

For the first time in his life, he could do what he liked. He hung up his oil pictures, which had only stood around in the cellar at home because Gitti didn't like them. He took along his record player and a few classical records, and before turning in he would pour himself a big glass of red wine. Never in his life had he felt so free.

Heinrich Scholl calls his time at the circus 'my first escape from home'.

He was in his mid-forties.

Brigitte Scholl continued to live in Ludwigsfelde as before. She worked in the beauty salon, went for walks with the dog, saw her girlfriends. Only once did she visit her husband at the circus. It was during a guest performance in Dresden. Heinrich Scholl had reserved special seats for his wife in the VIP lounge and bought fresh flowers for the circus caravan. But the world of the circus was alien to Brigitte Scholl and she found her husband changed beyond recognition. He seemed to feel at ease among these vagabonds, investing his skills in highwaymen and wild beasts. For the giraffes, he built a wagon tall enough to allow the long-necked animals to stand in transit; for the polar bears, he designed a new open-air enclosure and a pool. When his boss was away on holiday, he had all the tents and wagons resprayed—with black and white stripes like the circus zebras.

The head of Berolina was thrilled with his technical

manager. Heinrich Scholl was soon promoted to the executive board of East Germany's state circus and now had an office in their Berlin headquarters on Friedrichstrasse. He was popular and highly regarded; he was doing well. Once again he had followed a story-book trajectory. And once again he put an end to it.

He handed in his notice out of the blue. He says he made the decision one afternoon on Schöneweide Station. The station was too full for him; he realised that he no longer wanted to commute from Ludwigsfelde to Berlin every day. A spur-of-the-moment end to an adventure, and in Schöneweide, of all places, an utterly unremarkable suburb where nothing ever happened.

Scholl cleared out his circus caravan, took down his pictures and put them back in the cellar.

It was 1989. Scholl soon found new work. The town council of Ludwigsfelde was looking for a technical engineer for the municipal sports facilities: the public baths, the forest swimming pool, the sports grounds, the gyms. They were in a pitiful state, but the town's technical director, Scholl's boss, didn't seem to give a damn. He sat in the town hall reading *Neues Deutschland*, the official newspaper of the governing Socialist Unity Party, and regarded any criticism of his work as a betrayal of the grand socialist idea. Word had it he was unfireable. Heinrich Scholl avoided him as best he could. He set up a small office for himself at the public baths, mowed the lawn, had the showers fixed and the forest swimming pool and the sauna overhauled.

By now he was used to carving a niche for himself within society: in his own house, in among his deceased sister-in-law's West German furniture; at the naturist bathing spot between the birches; in his lamp workshop; in the circus caravan. But the niches were getting tighter. Scholl was no longer in Berlin negotiating with Swedes about a showpiece project for the biggest car works in East Germany; he was negotiating with a bored official about doing up a sauna in a small town.

The country was on its last legs.

WOWEREIT'S ADVICE

The night the Wall fell, Heinrich Scholl was in Josef Hospital in Potsdam. He had injured himself playing football and saw the images of that night on the television set above his hospital bed. He saw Günter Schabowski, a high-ranking party official, babbling something about a new travelling law; he saw his newly brave fellow-countrymen driving around West Berlin in their Trabants and falling sobbing into each other's arms; he saw helpless border guards. The man in the bed next to him was asleep—he remembers that; he would have liked someone to talk to, he says.

Three days later his son picked him up from hospital and drove him home, where time seemed to have stood still. There had been no Monday demonstrations and no peace services in Ludwigsfelde. The working-class town had no tradition of resistance—not under Hitler and not later either. Scholl's neighbours went to the works; his wife was busy with her customers and wasn't much interested in queuing for Jacobs coffee in West Berlin—she could get that in Intershop in Teltow.

Heinrich Scholl got his son to drive him into Berlin and

watched the queue at the border crossing at Oberbaum Bridge from the car. He was still on crutches and unable to mingle with his excited fellow-countrymen, but he didn't feel the need anyway. He was not euphoric; he was pensive. 'I knew the West from visiting my aunt, my mother and my sister-in-law,' he says. 'I wondered how on earth you were supposed to put all that together.'

Heinrich Scholl's attitude had always been one of cool detachment, but some didn't notice until now. His friend Dieter Fahle describes taking Scholl along to a dissenters' meeting in Gethsemane Church in Prenzlauer Berg—an area that was home to East Berlin's intellectuals, bohemians and activists—shortly before the Wall came down. It was September 1989, and the Monday demonstrations had just begun—non-violent demonstrations which were held at St Nicholas' church in Leipzig and would soon spread all over the country. More and more East German citizens were escaping to West Germany through Hungary each day, and the country was on the point of collapse. Everyone was wondering what was the worst that could happen—how dangerous resistance was, whether the military would get involved, whether there would be violence against demonstrators: shots fired, fatalities, war.

Dieter Fahle had just returned from a trip to Austria with his judo team and had read in the papers there that the Soviet army had incurred heavy losses in the war in Afghanistan. He concluded that Moscow's tanks would not be rolling into East Berlin. It was a somewhat complicated story—the judo team, the Austrian trip, Afghanistan, the Soviet army—but Dieter Fahle liked to draw big conclusions about global politics from minor news items. 'The Russians have shot all their rotten powder in Afghanistan!' he yelled at the civil rights activists. There was a discussion; everyone talked at once. At some point, Dieter Fahle looked around for Heinrich Scholl, who had been standing next to him just a moment before. Heinrich Scholl was gone.

Scholl says now that he can't stand such situations. When other people are brimming over with emotions, he feels nothing but a certain unease and the urge to withdraw. The first time he noticed this was at his father's funeral. Just a boy, he had stood among his relatives in the wooded cemetery of Ludwigsfelde. Everyone was crying; he couldn't. He tried to imagine this man, who had been so sick in the end that he hadn't even made it down the stairs to yell at him and beat him, now lying motionless over there in the coffin. Heinrich Scholl felt nothing: no grief, no pity, no pain—not even anger. He stood among all the weeping, black-clad people like a stranger.

Later too, when his mother left him by himself in Ludwigsfelde to move to West Berlin with Gerhard, he wasn't sad, disappointed or angry. He was merely surprised. He had firmly believed that she needed him—that by dint of his capability and his hard work, he had made himself indispensable. And then she upped and left to begin a new life without him. He couldn't make it add up. It made no sense to him.

It was the same when his mother died, in 1977. He had been told she was in a coma, and had gone to West Berlin to see her one last time. He had fought tooth and nail to get a ten-day entrance visa from the authorities, but only a day after he arrived, his mother was dead. He still had nine days left and decided to take the opportunity to visit Gitti's sister in Cologne.

Ursula sent him a plane ticket. He can still recount the details of this trip many years later: 'I get temporary ID at Tegel airport, spend seven days in Frechen, lovely house and nice husband, they show me around, specially nice trip to Bad Neuenahr, vineyards, terrific wine on old wine estate, flowers everywhere.' Not a word of grief, anger, hate or any other emotion.

Not long afterwards, he went once more to West Berlin. He organised his mother's cremation and the transportation of her ashes to Ludwigsfelde, and when he'd got everything done, he flew again to Gitti's sister in Cologne. This time he was taken to Aix-la-Chapelle, Bonn, Düsseldorf, Coblenz and Frankfurt.

Heinrich Scholl is a practical person, good at assessing things and analysing them. This quality had been of use to him many times in the course of his life, but never so much as in those autumn days of 1989. While his fellow-country-men were still reeling with delight and marching through the streets shouting, 'We are one people,' Heinrich Scholl put up his sore leg, watched the news, took note of what was going on around him and wondered what it might mean for him.

It was at this time that he met the West Berliner Klaus Wowereit.

They met in Mahlow, a small border town in Brandenburg and for decades the conduit through which the West Berliners' rubbish was channelled. This border crossing too was now open. You could walk from Mahlow to Lichtenrade and from Lichtenrade to Mahlow. The East Berliners went to collect their 'welcome money' in the West—a one-off payment of 100 marks that every East German was entitled to when visiting West Germany, the equivalent of about two months' rent in the East, and worth queuing for. The West Berliners went on Sunday-afternoon walks in the woods of Brandenburg.

Klaus Wowereit was in his mid-thirties, the youngest town councillor in all Berlin and pretty fed up with the administrative routine and the hierarchies in his party, the social democratic SPD. 'Everything had to work like a ring binder,' Wowereit writes in his autobiography. 'Click it open, file in, click it shut and there's an end to it. No surprises, for goodness' sake—nothing complicated that might confuse things.' The fall of the Berlin Wall had electrified him.

Klaus Wowereit lived in a completely different world from Heinrich Scholl, but he was in a similar position. He was stuck in a system. One November day in 1989 they came face to face: the tall, rangy Wowereit and the short, lively Scholl. They introduced themselves: 'I'm Klaus,' 'I'm Heiner.' Wowereit said he wanted to build up the SPD in

Brandenburg with bright new people. Heinrich Scholl said he was looking for a new mission.

He told the man from the West his story. How he'd negotiated with the Swedes and fled the car works, how he'd made lamps, built fireplaces, travelled the country with a circus and played ping pong with animal tamers, how he was now in charge of the public baths in Ludwigsfelde while his boss sat in the town hall reading *Neues Deutschland*. It wasn't a bad story. Scholl sounded like the hero of a picaresque novel.

Klaus Wowereit later became governing mayor of Berlin—and an icon of the gay rights movement, after coming out in the middle of the electoral campaign with the famous words: 'I'm gay and that's a good thing.' Today he prefers not to talk about Heinrich Scholl any more, but in his autobiography he writes about the exciting times back then, remarking at one point: 'The engineer Heinrich Scholl from Ludwigsfelde made a great impression.'

Helga Gerlich, a midwife by profession, campaigned alongside Wowereit for the SPD at that time. At the weekend, they would drive to Brandenburg with trestle tables, thermos flasks and trays of cake. 'We wanted to entice people,' Helga Gerlich explains. She says all the East Germans knew was the SED—the former governing communist party—and the party bloc. 'Social democracy was alien to them. Of course, they thought parties and elections were a scam.'

Heinrich Scholl was different from most people in the East, Helga Gerlich says—not broken, not stooped. 'He was

nice and friendly and really not at all like an East German,'
her husband says. 'I always wondered why people from the
East couldn't look you in the eyes. Heiner could. He held
himself straight.'

Heinrich Scholl says it was Wowereit who put him on
the right track. At their first meeting in Mahlow, he told
Scholl that men like him were going to be in demand; he
should take the initiative in Brandenburg and do something,
make something happen, take up an office, become district
administrator or mayor—now was the perfect time. Heinrich Scholl remembers asking: 'How?' And he remembers
Wowereit telling him that the only way of getting anywhere
in the West was through party structures.

One Sunday morning, a few days later, Heinrich Scholl
got in his Wartburg and drove to Christinendorf, a village
in Brandenburg with a few old farmsteads, a church with
a crooked steeple and a young vicar. The vicar was called
Steffen Reiche. He wore the full beard of a civil rights activ-
ist, gave political sermons and had not long since helped to
found social democracy in East Germany—by establishing
a branch of the SPD.

Reiche provided the party structure Klaus Wowereit had
been talking about.

The church was full, and the audience looked like the
one in Gethsemane Church—long-haired young men and
women, dressed in knitted sweaters and parkas. Heinrich
Scholl didn't fit in; he was much older than the others, wore
a pale trench coat and propped himself up on his crutch.

The vicar thought the Stasi had sent along their last man; people sitting nearby eyed him with suspicion. Scholl paid no attention; he took a seat on the aisle and listened to the sermon. When it was over and everybody left, he remained seated. Another man across the aisle from him also remained seated. He was the same age as Scholl and, with his moustache and crew-cut, just as much out of place. When this man walked up to the altar in search of the vicar, who had just vanished behind it, Heinrich Scholl hobbled after him.

Dieter Ertelt, the man from the other side of the aisle, was also from Ludwigsfelde, worked in the car factory, as Scholl had, and, like him, had had trouble with the state and wanted to be involved in the changes taking place in his country. He didn't know Heinrich Scholl. Here, in the church in Christinendorf, he set eyes on him for the first time.

Reiche told the two men to join the SPD, to set up a local branch of the party in Ludwigsfelde, enlist members and take part in the official 'round-table talks' being held around the country to discuss East Germany's future. That was about the extent of his advice, he says. He had stumbled into politics just as unprepared as Scholl and Ertelt—only a little earlier.

A few days later, Heinrich Scholl, Dieter Ertelt, Ertelt's wife and five other people from Ludwigsfelde set up the town's first local Social Democratic association since the Second World War. Heinrich Scholl, who had the best handwriting, drew up the deed. A few weeks later, the two men were sitting together at a round-table discussion and after a few months, they were both in the town hall. Heinrich Scholl became mayor; Dieter Ertelt was his deputy.

A photo from this time shows two middle-aged men wearing shirts open at the collar and leather bomber jackets with shoulder pads. Scholl is holding a piece of paper in his hand and reading from it, while Ertelt, his head on one side, is earnestly looking on. They look as if they're practising playing politicians.

Looking at the picture, you get a sense of what it must be like to slip into a new life overnight. It was happening all over East Germany at the time. Mayors and ministers and factory managers and editors-in-chief had to clear their desks from one day to the next to make room for people who seemed reliable enough to take up a new office in a new society. It was an historic chance, but it was also an experiment and no one could say how it would turn out—what the newfound power, the sudden success, the unexpected limelight might do to people who had never learnt to deal with it.

Dieter Fahle, Scholl's school friend, was on the round table in Zossen along with Heinrich Scholl. 'Scholli had the whole thing sussed from the beginning,' he says. 'Once, as we were driving home together, I said to him: "We'll be well out of all this before long anyhow." He said: "Not me, I'm going to stay."'

SILVER WEDDING

Heinrich Scholl was now mayor, the most important person in Ludwigsfelde, but he sometimes wasn't sure if that was really cause for joy. Sixty years had gone by since his parents had moved here, but the town was still the dump that his mother had so loathed. The munitions factory had given way to the car works; Adolf Hitler Strasse and Heinrich Himmler Strasse had been renamed after communists Ernst Thälmann and Wilhelm Pieck. The town hall was in a barracks where SS guards had once kept a watch on forced labourers; the motorway split the town down the middle, and the two records boasted by Ludwigsfelde were not necessarily something to be proud of: it had the largest single home-ownership district in East Germany and a bar which sold more beer than any other in the country. Its name was 'Sanssouci', but no one ever called it anything but 'the dive'.

The first summer after the Wall came down, the weekend trippers, glad to be able to get out of town at last, flocked across from West Berlin to the sewage farms of Brandenburg and spread out their picnic rugs. The old East German products were disappearing from the stores: in living rooms, black-and-white TVs were being swapped for colour sets; out on the streets, Trabants were being swapped for VWs; you came across the old car bodies at the roadside. The car works continued to produce its trucks, but nobody wanted to buy them any more, and everyone was anxiously wondering where things went from here. Young people were packing their suitcases and making off for the West in droves.

Frank left too. He was in his mid-twenties, an engineer by profession like his father. His mother, who had never left Ludwigsfelde for more than two weeks at a stretch, turned him out of the house in her friendly but resolute manner to ensure, as she put it, that he didn't end up having to 'put the lights out', like the last one to leave when everyone else has gone. Heinrich Scholl drove his son in the Wartburg Tourist to a refugee home in Hanover. The day he became mayor, Frank was camping in a gym among Eastern European refugees.

In all the excitement, Brigitte and Heinrich Scholl nearly forgot their twenty-fifth wedding anniversary. Silver wedding! At some point, long before the collapse of the Wall, the Scholls had signed up for a cruise to Cuba. Now the voucher was in their letter box: three weeks on the *Arkona*, East Germany's biggest cruise ship. They set sail in February 1990—a voyage across the ocean to the last socialist island, on board the last socialist ship. There were no longer any security checks. The officers, who had up until then had to make sure that no one jumped ship off the Azores to swim to the capitalist shore, were now serving piña coladas. The mood among the passengers was exuberant. Heinrich Scholl felt better than he had ever felt in his life.

When an English interpreter was wanted for a tour of the Azores, Heinrich Scholl stood at the front of the bus and translated for the other East Germans what the tour guide had to say about the islands' history, climate and volcanic eruptions. Scholl, who had learnt English at an adult education centre, didn't understand everything, but he talked and talked and let his fellow passengers toast him afterwards at the bar. Every evening, a competition of some kind was organised on the ship. Heinrich Scholl designed the best menu, managed the most hip bends, the most push-ups, the most pull-ups and won the prize for the best Mardi Gras costume. He won everything—every competition.

But he couldn't win over his wife.

Brigitte Scholl's husband could do what he liked; she acted as if she'd never expected anything else of him. When he first took up office as mayor, she had laid out suit, shirt and matching tie for him without a word. It was her only comment, her only way of showing recognition. On the cruise ship, Brigitte Scholl was usually already in bed when her husband was being fêted. She seldom drank more than a single glass of wine. The merrier and louder the others became, the more taciturn Brigitte Scholl was, until eventually she would withdraw to her cabin.

Twenty-five years ago, she had said yes in an East Berlin registry office. Ever since then, Heinrich Scholl had been trying to prove to her that she had made the right decision. But it was only ever the others around him who were impressed.

A POSITION OF AUTHORITY

Dieter Bartha was, you might say, Ludwigsfelde's first West German visitor. He was the deputy mayor of Paderborn, and Paderborn was one of the towns newly twinned with Ludwigsfelde. Bartha still remembers his first visit in July 1990, he says, because it was at a time when he was fighting to get the dilapidated old town hall in Paderborn replaced by a new one. 'Then I arrived in Ludwigsfelde with my town clerk, and when we stood outside the Siberian shack where Scholl had his seat, I knew I could forget my new town hall.'

Scholl's office had barred windows and a leaky roof; a gutter took the place of a urinal in the men's toilets, and when the gas stove was lit in the winter, the air was blue. There were no computers; only old typewriters. The secretary was snappish; the many town hall employees, who did no one knew quite what, seemed wary. The hall of residence belonging to the car works, where the visitors from Paderborn were put up, resembled a barracks. 'For breakfast there were bread roll halves,' says Dieter Bartha. 'They'd been pre-buttered too.'

The East was just as the West German had imagined it. Only Heinrich Scholl didn't fit the picture. He wasn't a bitter, pig-headed politician or ideologue; he was well dressed, open-minded and brimming with energy. He welcomed emissaries from West German companies and the state government, came up with suggestions about what route the motorway should take and decided the fate of many senior Stasi figures, army members and teachers.

Dieter Bartha had been treasurer of the financial committee of the German Association of Cities and Municipalities for a long time and got to know a great many mayors from the new federal states in the years following the collapse of the Wall—'but never a fellow like Scholl,' he says. Scholl was possessed by incredible fervour—visionary fervour, even. Every time Bartha came to Ludwigsfelde from Paderborn, something new had been completed. 'Heinrich Scholl,' he says, 'was the best thing that could have happened to that town.'

Dieter Ertelt, Scholl's deputy, has a photo of the old mayoral shack hanging in his kitchen, so fond are his memories of those times in the town hall with the man he had first met in the small church in Brandenburg. Scholl was in charge of the practical side of things: construction, investments, funding; Ertelt saw to formal matters: finances, budgets, schools, the administrative authority. 'A good division of labour,' Ertelt says. 'We didn't have a clue, but we made a good team. Heiner was very companionable, very friendly. There was no wheeling and dealing and eating out at the Italian restaurant in those days. It wasn't about jobs; it was about changing things.'

Rainer Fischer came to Ludwigsfelde from Berlin at the beginning of the nineties. His first impression was: a dump, a dormitory town. 'There was nothing but the motorway,' he says. 'The people all knew each other from the car works, all went about on bikes and didn't have a good word to say about Berliners. On one house I saw a poster saying, "Fuck off, Berlin meatball!"'

Fischer was a bio-geneticist in Adlershof, Berlin, until he was officially instructed to scale down his own institute and lay off two hundred of the five hundred employees. When he had finished doing that, he was offered a post as managing director of a construction business. Ludwigsfelde was his first project—and his biggest. In Potsdamer Strasse alone, Fischer had four hundred council flats built; business parks for Mercedes, MTU and various logistics companies were to follow. Nationwide, sixty-four applicants entered the tender to build Volkswagen's new logistics centre, but Ludwigsfelde's bid was accepted. 'Scholl brought in the investors,' Fischer says. 'His standard slogan was: "We're the town that the Paris–Moscow motorway passes through."'

Heinrich Scholl was a natural. He could negotiate with politicians just as well as with business people. He reduced the trade tax rate by half. He used up all the funding at his disposal for the reconstruction of the East—and often that of the neighbouring municipalities as well. Each year, millions of euros were set aside for the development of villages and towns in the East, but at the end of the year, there was always money over. Scholl took that money. If the federal state said it didn't have the human resources to get the plan under way before the year was over, he offered to take on the construction planning and the management himself.

The town south of Berlin was soon regarded as an East German economic miracle, a symbol of the economic recovery of the new federal states. While the neighbouring municipalities withered, Ludwigsfelde flourished. Heinrich Scholl had the old Nazi shack torn down and a new glass town hall built; he had the motorway raised on stilts, the lanes widened, noise barriers put up. He invited the architecture enthusiast Prince Charles to his town, shook hands with Chancellor Gerhard Schröder and his successor Angela Merkel, and whenever the premier of Brandenburg was in want of good news from his needy state, he drove to Ludwigsfelde and inaugurated something new with Heinrich Scholl.

Three times Heinrich Scholl was voted mayor. When he took up office, he was forty-seven years old and his son was just moving out. When he stepped down, eighteen years later, he was in his sixties, with grandchildren. For a politician from the new federal states, his term of office was record-breakingly long.

There are several stories about fallen heroes of the German autumn of revolution, some of them bizarre. Ibrahim Böhme, the first leader of East Germany's newly founded Social Democratic Party, was revealed after only

a few months to have been a Stasi spy who had invented
the bulk of his biography. Wolfgang Schnur of Democratic
Awakening, the man who got Angela Merkel her first political
office, was expelled from the party that he had founded
himself because of his Stasi connections. He later insulted
a judge, and was found guilty of delaying bankruptcy; and
for a while he disappeared and was believed missing, until it
was confirmed that he died early in 2016 in Vienna. Jochen
Wolf, construction minister of Brandenburg, lost his post
over a dishonest property deal and wound up in jail a few
years later because he had tried to hire a contract killer to
murder his wife. Others lost their jobs over corruption or
sex scandals.

Heinrich Scholl was familiar with these stories and knew
how easy it would be to fall into temptation and lose all that
he had gone to such pains to build up. 'Oh boy, what a lot
I was offered,' he says. 'Envelopes with 35,000 Swiss francs
and what have you.' Scholl didn't trip up. He resisted temptation or else legalised it. In his very first legislative term,
the city council of Ludwigsfelde granted him certain exemp-
tions as mayor—he was permitted to attend lunches and
dinners paid for by business connections, for example, and
even to accept invitations go on trips with them. This was
one of the tips he had received from his colleagues from the
West German twin towns. He was quick on the uptake for
an East German, taking especial note of the pointers given
to him over a glass of red wine of an evening. One of these
was never to make a proposal to the city council until you

were sure of having the majority on your side. The parties of Ludwigsfelde were usually in agreement anyway, but when it was looking close, Heinrich Scholl would sit down at the telephone and ring every last delegate until he was sure he had enough votes.

At some meetings, when a topic became the subject of controversial debate and Scholl sensed that the majority were turning against him, he would get up and leave the room, saying that he felt unwell. On occasion he would begin to cry. The man who hadn't been able to shed a single tear at his father's grave broke down and wept when the conservation league tried to prevent him from felling hundred-and-fifty-year-old pitch pines to build an access road. Everyone was against him: the minister, the conservationists—even his own head of construction sat there in silence. Heinrich Scholl's tears helped. His opponents exchanged looks of stunned shock. One of them said: 'Ach, Herr Scholl, don't take it so personally.' But of course he took it personally, Heinrich Scholl replied.

He had to win—to be better than the others. Even now.

Jutta Abromeit, a local reporter on the *Märkische Allgemeine* newspaper, once accompanied him to three different appointments in one day: an old-age-pensioners' gathering in the morning, an opening ceremony at midday and a city council meeting in the evening. On each occasion, Heinrich Scholl raised the same topic, but he varied his approach, twisting his arguments, altering them so that they were perfectly tailored to the group in question. Anything

contradictory he left out. He seemed to be one hundred per
cent convinced of what he was saying every time, but at the
third and final appointment, Jutta Abromeit says, he caught
her eye and then turned quickly away. 'He realised that I'd
seen through him.'

Scholl, she says, could manipulate people, win them over
to his side and implicate them in his arguments like key witnesses. 'Isn't that so, Frau Abromeit?' he had kept asking.
Mid-speech, in front of everyone else.

He managed to hold people captive and yet remain amaz-
ingly vague at the same time. In the local newsroom, he was
renowned for starting sentences and not finishing them. 'It
was terribly hard to quote him in an article,' Jutta Abromeit
says. 'I only ever had half-sentences on my notepad.'

There are countless pictures of Heinrich Scholl at this
time: Scholl with SPD leader Hans-Jochen Vogel; Scholl
with the premier of Brandenburg, Manfred Stolpe;
Scholl with the landlady of the 'Old Inn'; Scholl with the
minister of social affairs, Regine Hildebrandt; Scholl with
the head of Mercedes; Scholl with young people on a TV
panel discussion; Scholl pulling a beer; Scholl in a digger;
Scholl in a construction pit; Scholl with a group of appren-
tices; Scholl celebrating the town's birthday; Scholl cutting
the first sod for a new business park; Scholl at the new city
archives; Scholl at a New Year's reception; Scholl with the
boxer Henry Maske; Scholl with a topless snake charmer;
Scholl at the inauguration of a crèche; Scholl with the minister of sport and education, Steffen Reiche; Scholl with the

minister of finance, Hans Eichel; Scholl laying the foundation stone for five town houses; Scholl at the opening of the six-lane motorway; Scholl with guests from Ludwigsfelde's twin towns; Scholl playing football; Scholl at the firemen's ball; Scholl on the jury of the Miss Ludwigsfelde competition. He was everywhere—down in a sewage drain and up on stage with the heir to the British throne.

The pictures bear witness to a fairy-tale ascent. In the early photos, his hair is short, his gaze boyish; he wears short-sleeved shirts—no tie, no jacket—and doesn't know what to do with his arms. He is always shorter than everybody else; it looks as if he is crouching or sitting or playing football with giants. Bustle and laughter cover up his insecurity. Heinrich Scholl plays the clown. Sometimes his gestures seem practised, casual, and then suddenly he'll be standing stripped to the waist next to Mardi Gras revellers or holding a toy pistol to his treasurer's head. He is ever-present and never tired. In most of the photos you can see how proud he is at having got so far. At times, though, you can sense his fear of losing everything.

NEW FRIENDS

Brigitte Scholl now saw her husband more on billboards and up on stage than at home. Her son was grown-up and lived in the West. The two most important people in her life were starting all over again, while she stayed at home with her dead sister's furniture and carried on running her beauty salon. There were new products and a new currency: the standard treatment had once cost twenty East German marks; in 1990, the price switched to twenty deutsch-marks; later it would be twenty euros. Otherwise, not much changed.

Brigitte Scholl's daily routine was largely dictated by the beauty salon and the dog. Every morning, between five and half past, she got up and took Ursus for a walk; at eight her first customer arrived; at twelve her lunch break began— and with it her daily walk in the woods; at two it was back to the salon until six o'clock. Then it was suppertime, and shortly before turning in, she would take the dog for a last walk round the block.

She still had a brown cocker spaniel, just like the one she had been given by a boyfriend back in the days when she was a young woman with half of Ludwigsfelde at her feet. When the first dog had died, she had bought a new one that looked just the same: brown wavy coat, floppy ears, a trusting look. Brigitte Scholl had lost her mother and her sister; her son had moved out, and her husband was never at home, but the dog was a fixture.

She clung to the things she knew—the things familiar to her. She had never liked leaving Ludwigsfelde and that didn't change when the Wall came down. She made a few trips with her husband—to France, Italy, the south of England—but she felt most at ease at home, in her small, self-contained world: the house, the salon, the bathing spot. Ludwigsfelde was her haven; she felt safe there. And she didn't have to leave town to get to know the new world. The new world came to her.

Helga Gerlich, the social democrat from Lichtenrade, met Brigitte Scholl in the summer of 1990. 'After a party function, Heiner said: "You're coming back with me for a change."' They drove to the house in Rathenau Strasse. Brigitte Scholl came to the door, asked them in, showed them round the house and apologised for her sister's old furniture. Helga Gerlich says she liked the house far better than her own; everything was so tidy and well-kept. Some women, she says, are interior designers by nature. 'Brigitte was one of them. Her star sign is orderly Virgo. That was in evidence all over the house.'

Helga Gerlich went back to Brigitte Scholl as a customer. Her salon prices were lower than in Berlin. 'I said to her:

"You must put your prices up, if you want to make a go of it."' Brigitte Scholl said: 'Helga, I can't take more money from my customers. They don't have that much.'

Gerlich liked the dedicated mayor, who only a short while before had been building giraffe wagons in the circus, and she liked his modest wife. But above all, she admired their relationship, which seemed so much more egalitarian than her own. Heinrich Scholl might have been the most powerful man in town, but when his wife called him, he came running. Heiner laid the table, did the shopping, filled up the car, mowed the lawn and took the dog round the block. Without a word of protest. Even if he happened to be busy, he didn't ask whether it couldn't wait until later, but dropped everything to carry out his wife's instructions. A dream! Brigitte Scholl could even ring her husband in the middle of an important meeting and dictate the shopping list to him over the phone without his complaining. In the evenings he would bring her flowers.

'I always had the impression that Brigitte and Heiner understood each other without words,' Helga Gerlich says. 'They never argued—really, not ever. Brigitte once told me he was a good lover, very good even. I envied the Scholls their marriage and was always saying to my husband: "Look at Heiner."' Helga Gerlich was firmly convinced that the Scholls' marriage was exemplary. A modern relationship, a model for the future.

Klaus Wowereit, too, enjoyed visiting Brigitte and Heinrich. He often took his mother along. She would lie on Gitti's

salon bed and let Gitti apply masks and give her neck massages and pedicures, while her son discussed the future of
social democracy in the kitchen with Heiner Scholl. Wowereit was annoyed by the hierarchies and power games of the
old men in his constituency. 'I was on my way up the ladder
and he was already thinking of chucking it all in,' Heinrich
Scholl says. Wowereit was often in Ludwigsfelde at that
time, at the local SPD association or having dinner at Gitti
and Heiner's. He was trying to understand the problems in
the East, to get to know the people there. If it got late, he
would stay the night in the spare room.

'Heiner and Brigitte liked entertaining and everything
was always prepared for us when we came,' Helga Gerlich
says. 'Brigitte couldn't help herself; she was a perfectionist.'
Once, they had celebrated New Year's Eve together in the
restaurant at Siethen and gone ice bathing on New Year's
morning. In summer, their new friends from West Berlin
joined the Scholls for naturist swimming at the gravel pit.
The big public bathing area was crowded, but the small private spot between the birches was as empty as ever, reserved
for Gitti and her group of bathers. They spread out rugs,
undressed, sunbathed, swam. Sometimes Wowereit went
with them—Klaus, as they now knew him.

Brigitte Scholl moved with astonishing self-confidence in
these new social circles: she held dinner parties, went the
rounds at receptions, brought people together. Sometimes
the district administrator was among the guests, sometimes
an entrepreneur from Cologne or Switzerland. When she

rang her friends, the first thing she'd tell them was which big shots she'd met lately and when Heiner could be seen on which talk show. She bought him suits and shirts and ties, and put together an outfit for him every morning.

Joachim Lehmann*, a former schoolmate of Brigitte Scholl, whom she had met again at a class reunion, now had regular invitations to parties at the Scholls'. Lehmann was a psychologist by profession, tall, bearded, eloquent—someone you could be seen with. Other people, however—old friends—were struck off the guest list. Brigitte Scholl had always surrounded herself with certain people only, but now that her husband was mayor, she became even choosier. Her girlfriends still received invitations, but Brigitte Scholl liked to dictate what they were to wear and how they were to behave. Gitti, the beauty queen of Ludwigsfelde, couldn't bear it if eyebrows weren't plucked or hair not properly set. Women who turned up without make-up were sat on a salon chair and painted until she was satisfied. Rainer Fischer, Scholl's Berlin business friend, got to know Brigitte Scholl on a short trip to Zurich. Hardly had they arrived at the hotel when she looked Fischer's wife up and down and took her off to her room 'to show her how to make herself up properly'. His wife returned looking like a paint box, Fischer says.

There were certain things that Brigitte Scholl preferred not to leave to chance. She would take charge, giving her friends presents, making doctors' appointments for customers and organising lifts to the practice. She bought concert and theatre tickets. Every book she read, every film she liked, she had to recommend. When she visited the vet and his wife with Ursus, she set about rehanging the pictures in their living room. There was often something pushy and overbearing about her solicitude; it was hard to escape it. This led to misunderstandings—and sometimes to the breaking-off of relations.

The friendship between Heinrich Scholl and Hans Streck suffered a rift during Brigitte Scholl's preparations for a belated party to celebrate the silver wedding. She had invited half the town and drawn up a tightly packed program: cocktail reception, lunch, dinner and a tour of the new Daimler works. It was to be a party that people would remember all their lives; everything had to be perfect. Including the guests' outfits.

The first phone call to the Strecks in North Rhine Westphalia came soon after the invitation. Brigitte Scholl wanted to know from Hans Streck's wife what she was thinking of wearing.

A dress, she said. What else?

Brigitte Scholl explained that one dress wasn't enough. The party was going to go on from morning until night; it would be in several stages. You didn't wear the same to a cocktail reception as you wore to a dinner. And, of course, you couldn't turn up to a tour of the Daimler works in your little black number.

Hans Streck was Heinrich Scholl's best school friend; he'd known Brigitte Scholl's nagging for many years and he hated it. But this time it was worse. Brigitte Scholl rang daily with new instructions for his wife. She must remember to bring suitable shoes and jewellery—and a jacket in case it turned chilly. Again and again the phone rang. In the end his wife stopped picking it up and announced that she wasn't going to attend the party for the world. Her husband didn't even try to persuade her. He rang the Scholls to explain. Heinrich Scholl said he was sorry; Gitti hadn't meant it that way. Brigitte Scholl did not apologise. Hans Streck and his wife stayed at home.

By and large, Brigitte Scholl tended to focus her attention on women, but occasionally men too came under her scrutiny. A Swiss business partner of her husband was asked out of the blue whether he smoked; she'd noticed he had such yellow teeth. A local councillor was warmly advised to get the nape of his neck shaved. Her remarks were poison—small, well-measured injections, with which she could silence an entire table. Most of all, she liked to make a spectacle of her husband. If they had friends round and the men wanted to watch football, she would say that Heiner had to wash the car first. She'd get him to cut the hedge, and if she wasn't satisfied with the result, she'd have the gardener in to redo it the next day. Customers overheard her ordering him to mow the lawn— 'and that means now, not this evening.'

Even the premier of Brandenburg got to witness the way the mayor's wife treated her husband. Heinrich Scholl had given a speech at the Ludwigsfelde Cultural Centre and returned from the stage to the table where Manfred Stolpe,

Rainer Speer and Matthias Platzeck were sitting—Brandenburg's top squad. The audience was still applauding. A state
secretary said, 'Great, Heiner, terrific,' and picked up a bottle of red wine to pour Scholl a glass. Brigitte Scholl covered
his glass with her hand and said: 'My husband has already
had a glass.' The secretary of state said that after his fantastic speech, Scholl deserved another one. Brigitte Scholl said
she thought not: he'd said 'er' too often for that.

Brigitte Scholl loved to humiliate her husband. People
knew this. If Heinrich Scholl got to the bathing spot a bit
late, his naturist friends would joke that he must have had to
wash the floor first. Once he turned up at the local paper's
annual football match without any trainers. His wife had
refused to let him leave before all the chores had been done,
and he had slipped out of the house with no shoes on. Any
greater domestic revolt than that was beyond Heinrich
Scholl's power.

The Ludwigsfelde reporter Jutta Abromeit once wit-
nessed the mayor attempting to resist his wife's authority.
Scholl had just planted a lime tree in front of the oldest
restaurant in Ludwigsfelde and was standing together with
a few guests over a beer. It was a warm summer's day. Jutta
Abromeit was talking to Heinrich Scholl when his wife
appeared and announced: 'We're going home.'

The mayor pretended he hadn't heard and carried on
talking to the journalist. He didn't even turn round.

His wife waited quite some time and then she left.

At the beginning of his term of office, Brigitte Scholl

often accompanied her husband to events and opening cer-
emonies. Later, she preferred to stay at home. She hated
standing around at his side like a vase. The social democrats
from West Berlin, whom she had liked, hardly showed up
in Ludwigsfelde now anyway. Klaus Wowereit had become
mayor of Berlin in 2001 and was busier than ever. Brigitte
Scholl no longer told Helga Gerlich about her amazing sex
life, but complained that she was often alone. When Heiner
came home late, she said, he smelt of alcohol—she didn't
like that. If he didn't return at all, she chased him up with
phone calls. When her psychologist friend, Joachim Lehmann, had appointments with patients in Ludwigsfelde, she
would insist he drop in afterwards 'just for a minute'. Then
she would prepare an enormous meal and play the hostess,
just as she had once done with her schoolmates when she
was still the beautiful, rich hairdressers' daughter. Joachim
Lehmann says he felt sorry for Brigitte Scholl.

She rang her girlfriends every day, telling them what she
was reading and what programs they mustn't miss. She knew
every new diet, every type of treatment, every doctor in the
area, every new restaurant, every new shop and every joke.
One of her jokes went like this: 'What does a woman do
with her arse in the morning?—She sends him to work.' At
this point, Brigitte Scholl would pause. Then she would say,
'I've already sent mine off,' and half kill herself laughing.

Brigitte Scholl felt overshadowed by her husband's
increasing status and importance and fought to reassert herself. She needed a public platform of her own, a mission,

and found it at the Ludwigsfelde Women's House. Brigitte Scholl wanted to help there, but in such a way that it was noticed—and noticed all over town. She organised something completely new: an Advent market, with profits to go to the Women's House.

For weeks, Brigitte Scholl and her friend Heike collected old things to sell. It was a time when the people of Ludwigsfelde were revamping everything and keen to get rid of their old East German things. The first Advent market under the auspices of the mayor's wife was held on the cinema forecourt. Brigitte Scholl welcomed her guests, her husband at her side. Then the two of them went from stall to stall like a royal couple, distributing smiles and good words. Brigitte Scholl walked half a pace in front of her husband; she was in command. After that, the Advent market took place every year—on the big square in front of the town hall, or in the cultural centre. A choir sang, Brandenburg artists sold their pictures and woodwork, and a local party leader dressed up as Father Christmas. Brigitte Scholl had found a new role for herself. She was now the town's charity queen, a kind of Lady Di of Ludwigsfelde. She arranged to meet heads of companies, told them about the affliction of women who were abused by their husbands—and wouldn't leave until cheques had been signed. In her salon was a little money box. Whenever her customers wanted to give her a tip, she would say: 'No, thank you, but if you had a small donation for the Women's House...'

AT THE PEAK

But there was no stopping Heinrich Scholl either. The people of Ludwigsfelde had taken to calling him Napoleon, because he was so short and so ambitious—the five-foot-four world conqueror. It wasn't enough for him to be the mayor of a showpiece town. He knew he could do that. He needed new challenges. In the past, he had done gymnastics and rowed; now he ran and played football—and eventually he took up mountaineering.

It was triggered by a remark made by his wife. They had gone to the Tyrol on a hiking holiday and were sitting outside a mountain hut in the sun when a man came past on his way down from Mount Ortler, the highest mountain in South Tyrol. Brigitte Scholl asked him how old he was. Seventy, said the mountain climber. Brigitte Scholl said to her husband: 'Heiner, did you hear that? The man's already seventy and he's been up Ortler. You wouldn't dare do that.'

Heinrich Scholl had a new goal.

His climb began at six in the morning; at 10.30 he had reached the peak of Mount Ortler, and he got back to the hut that afternoon. Hardly had he returned from his holidays when he registered with the German Alpine Club. He went on week-long mountaineering courses, learnt climbing techniques, went jogging in the woods with sandbags in his rucksack and immediately booked another course for the following year. In his notes on his life, Heinrich Scholl dedicates twenty-three closely written pages to the subject of mountaineering. The sentence 'I'm at the end of my strength' crops up repeatedly, but it is invariably followed by the reward: 'a terrific sunrise'. Twenty-three pages of endless torment and stunning sunrises.

Heinrich Scholl's most important companion in this phase of his life was his mountain guide, Wolfgang. When Heinrich Scholl had time off, he no longer went on holiday with his wife; he went mountain climbing with Wolfgang. When Wolfgang said, 'Now you're ready for Mont Blanc,' Heinrich Scholl's life had meaning again. When Wolfgang said, 'We must keep going,' he kept going.

He often thought: It's not possible, I can't take any more. But it always was possible. And that was precisely what appealed to him about mountaineering: 'The challenge to be self-assertive,' he says. 'It's not just torture; you come close to death. You realise you're not a weakling and you're so proud of yourself.'

Heinrich Scholl climbed Kilimanjaro, Aconcagua and Mont Blanc, and nearly made it up Everest. He climbed 7200 metres without an oxygen cylinder. Once his toenails froze off; once he was almost snowbound; once he thought he was going to die. But nothing was ever high enough for the man from Ludwigsfelde. There was a joke going around town in those days: 'Why did Heinrich Scholl climb Kilimanjaro? —Because he wanted to be the tallest for once.'

Steffen Reiche accompanied Heinrich Scholl up Kilimanjaro. The vicar and co-founder of the East German SPD was now minister of sport in Brandenburg and a marathon runner. Whenever the men saw each other at meetings, they would compare records. On one such occasion, Steffen Reiche had told Heinrich Scholl to let him know if he ever planned to tackle Kilimanjaro. A few months later, Scholl rang Reiche and said he was ready. He had already got a group together, but they could do with one more participant. Reiche agreed, but then let things slide a bit, ordered his visa too late and didn't collect it from the post office in time.

Heinrich Scholl was furious when Steffen Reiche rang him to say he was standing outside the post office, which had shut half an hour before. Reiche almost remembers Scholl's fit of rage better than the climb up Kilimanjaro—that and the fact that Scholl ended up finding a solution. The branch manager of the post office was chair of the Ludwigsfelde handball club. Scholl rang the club and the man came to the post office, opened it up and dug out the letter containing Steffen Reiche's visa.

They flew to Nairobi via Amsterdam, drove to Kruger National Park and finally walked to the foot of the mountain. The climb took several days. In his notes, Heinrich Scholl recalls 'the terribly steep volcanic cones', 'the view over the craters', 'the twenty-metre glacier face' and, of course, 'a terrific sunrise'. Steffen Reiche still recalls it. 'I felt like a ninety-five-year-old being pushed out onto the balcony by his carer,' he says. 'We were told, two breaths, one step, but none of that was any help. My legs just couldn't go any further.'

When they reached the top at six in the morning, Heinrich Scholl took from his rucksack a small red-and-white flag bearing the coat of arms of Brandenburg. He stuck it in the sand and the two politicians had their photos taken by the mountain guide, each in turn and then together. But although it was Scholl who had carried the flag to the top of the highest mountain in Africa, only one of the photos made it into the *Bild* newspaper—that of the minister of sport, Steffen Reiche.

Brigitte Scholl was now alone at home more than ever. Alone on holiday too. On one occasion she joined a tour group to Morocco; another time she tried to find someone to accompany her on a trip to Turkey. But no one had the time—or else no one could contemplate spending two weeks with Gitti. Luckily, she had her salon and the dog and a nice neighbour who put out the bins for her, drove her to the garden centre to buy plants and chauffeured her to doctors' appointments in Berlin. In the evenings she watched TV or read novels with titles like *Feathers in the Wind*, *Ways of Love* or *Flowers in the Rain*. Her girlfriends asked her round, but Brigitte Scholl rarely went. She preferred to be hostess herself.

One day, Brigitte Scholl found an anonymous letter in the post box informing her that her husband was having an affair with a town hall employee. She had already suspected something of the kind and wasn't surprised, but she did feel profoundly humiliated. Pride and munificence were fundamental to Brigitte Scholl's character, underpinning her status in town, her good standing. Nothing was more important to her than what people in town thought of her; she had learnt that from her mother. Now her reputation was ruined.

The rumours were true: Heinrich Scholl says he was sixty when he fell in love for the first time in his life. Properly in love. He had married his wife because she was beautiful and wealthy and needed a father for her child. It had been a marriage of reason. His new relationship was far from reasonable. The woman was more than twenty years younger than Scholl; she had a child and a husband. Like Heinrich Scholl, she worked in the town hall. She was his employee; he was her boss.

Now all he wanted was to be together with her. He thought she looked like the film star Julia Roberts—especially when she laughed. Sometimes he would wait in his car in a side street after work and they would go out to eat in a country pub, or else drive to a small house on the lake, to which Scholl had the keys from a friend.

In the town hall, word spread fast, of course. Scholl was mayor. The deceived husband rang his office if his wife didn't get home from work on time. She couldn't cope with the pressure for long and put an end to the relationship.

Brigitte Scholl reacted in her own way to her husband's infidelity. She didn't turn him out; that would only have damaged her reputation further. She went to Klotz Funeral Directors and bought herself an urn grave with a small marble slab, which was to bear her name. The grave was to be for her alone. Her son Frank was to give the eulogy at her funeral.

Frank and her friend Inge in Anklam were the only ones to be let in on her plans. They had to promise Brigitte Scholl that her husband would never stand at her grave.

THERAPY

Heinrich Scholl fell ill. Like his father before him, he'd had problems with his stomach all his life. His mother-in-law had given him 'rolling cures', and during his time at the car works he had sometimes been off sick for weeks on end. But it had never been as bad as after the break-up with his mistress. He had unbearable pains, had to leave meetings, was obliged to wear incontinence pads and was losing a lot of blood. A doctor diagnosed ulcerative colitis, a chronic inflammatory bowel disease whose causes are largely unknown. Genetic background can have an impact, but so can stress.

Scholl ran from one doctor to the next and tried out various drugs. Nothing was any use. A professor in Berlin's Westend Clinic told him: 'We can't put you to rights here, Herr Scholl. There's nothing I can do.' He prescribed a spell in a health resort on Lake Tegern, in southern Germany. Good walking there, the professor said—and a good therapist too.

Heinrich Scholl had never had therapy. He envisaged a red couch with an analyst sitting at the head, like in a

Hollywood film. The thought of lying on this couch and talking about his worries seemed ridiculous to him. But he had no choice; he was no longer able to go to work, he was losing more and more weight, and the doctor had told him that the inflammation could develop into cancer. The mayor of Ludwigsfelde turned his affairs over to his deputy and set off for Bavaria.

His first therapy appointment was shortly after his arrival. There was a couch, just like in the movies, and an analyst. 'She was about forty—good-looking,' says Scholl. 'I thought: "She's far too young."'

He talked about his work as mayor—how he had brought the town forward over the past fifteen years, and how difficult it had been, how he had to fight every step of the way, on his own every time, especially with his most recent project, a twenty-million-euro thermal spa which was to replace the old public baths. His life was one long battle: Heinrich against the rest of the world. Scholl talked and talked, because he certainly could talk, but after a while the therapist asked: 'Are you happily married, Herr Scholl?'

He said: 'I'm married, but I wouldn't say happily.'

The therapist asked why. He shrugged his shoulders. He didn't know. He'd been married to Gitti for forty years and sensed that something wasn't right—that they were growing further and further apart, that he didn't like being with her any longer and that she didn't like being with him. But he had never thought about what the reasons might be.

The therapist said maybe he'd find it easier to think about

if he wrote down everything that came into his head on slips of paper. That was his homework: 'Write down what bothers you about your wife, Herr Scholl.'

Heinrich Scholl turned up at the next session bearing little slips of paper with notes on them. He had written:

Nannies me.

Doesn't let me hang up my pictures.

Has a cleaning mania.

Treats me like a small child.

No love any more!

There were a lot of notes. Heinrich Scholl had to read each one out loud—every last reproach. It was easier than he had expected. He says it was only then that he understood how his wife's constant reprimands had destroyed him inside. 'I couldn't react. Not ever,' he says.

'Herr Scholl, you put up with all this. Do you ever slam your fist down on the table at home? Have you ever really yelled at her?' the therapist asked.

'No, I can't. I'm not the type,' said Scholl.

'Then you only have one chance of recovery. You must take some time off, or leave altogether.'

It wasn't advice; it was an order. Heinrich Scholl returned to Ludwigsfelde determined not to put up with any more of his wife's high-handedness. But it wasn't easy. When she instructed him to rake the leaves on the lawn in the morning before he left for work, he said he could just as well do it in the evening. She said nothing. When Scholl got home that evening, she had raked the lawn herself. In return, she hadn't made him any supper: his plate was empty. He went up to his room without eating. He was strong-willed; he could stick it out. That was his way of looking at it, his way of dealing with it. The house of the exemplary Scholls was witnessing scenes reminiscent of *The War of the Roses*. On one occasion, however, when there had been no supper for a whole week because Scholl had got back from a meeting half an hour late, he packed his suitcase and moved to a friend's flat in Berlin. It was his second escape from home. When he returned after six weeks, his wife seemed pleased. She made him meals, called him 'darling'.

Three weeks later, everything was back to normal.

'She had this way of going on; she simply wouldn't leave off,' says her friend Karin Singer. When Heinrich Scholl came back from the health resort, it had been particularly marked. Suddenly someone was resisting her—challenging her. 'He'd had psychological counselling there and had changed a lot. He thought he no longer had to put up with everything from Gitti. But he simply couldn't assert himself. I said to her: "Just leave him."'

On one occasion, when he had to go to hospital because of his intestinal troubles, she visited him there and was turned away with the words: '*You're* my disease.' Gitti was hurt. But she wasn't prepared to change.

Heinrich Scholl was, nevertheless, able to persuade his wife to accompany him to couples therapy. A friend had told him of a vicar in Berlin who offered marriage counselling. Brigitte Scholl wasn't keen, but a vicar sounded less menacing to her than a therapist. And Berlin was far enough away; there was no risk of anyone in Ludwigsfelde getting wind of it. She put on a nice dress and let her husband drive her to the capital.

The vicar greeted the couple. Then he suggested that he begin by speaking to each of the partners individually. Heinrich Scholl, who had made the appointment, was to go first; his wife should wait outside the door until she was called in.

This is perfectly standard procedure in couples therapy. The therapist likes the partner who has sought help to begin by explaining his or her reasons for doing so. Then it's the turn of the other partner, and finally both are asked in together to find solutions to their problems.

Brigitte Scholl, however, saw only that her husband was being favoured. She was at this time a woman of sixty who had never learnt to talk about her problems. Her parents had drowned their worries in alcohol; her sister had washed hers down with pills. All she had to cling to was her authority. Now she sat outside the door, imagining her husband and the vicar hatching a plan to get her over a barrel. She thought it was a conspiracy, a put-up job. When the therapist called her in, she said: 'My husband has paid you, I presume?' Then she turned on her heel, leaving the two men sitting there.

Afterwards, on the phone to her friend Inge, she told her indignantly about the trip to Berlin. She and Heiner had been to see a vicar who wanted to accuse her of being task-master-in-chief at home. Inge Karther says she had always advised Brigitte not to fence her husband in so much; she had even told her once in his presence. 'But anyone who knew her realised that there wasn't actually any point. She didn't mean any harm; it's just the way she was.' There was no changing her.

Heinrich Scholl's attempt to salvage his marriage had failed. But separation was no more an option for him than it was for his wife. In this respect they were in agreement. Brigitte Scholl wanted to keep up appearances. Heinrich Scholl didn't want to jettison all that he had worked hard to obtain in life. They were inseparable.

RETIREMENT

The less say Heinrich Scholl had at home, the more power-conscious he became at work. His portrait in oils now hung in the municipal museum. His office in the new town hall was at least three times the size of his old barracks office. He was used to getting his way and regarded any form of opposition as a personal attack.

'Scholl was the uncrowned king of Ludwigsfelde,' says journalist Jutta Abromeit.

Dieter Ertelt, Scholl's longstanding deputy, had taken early retirement. This had not a little to do with his boss. Scholl preferred to do everything himself, says Dieter Ertelt—and always right away. 'If he was determined to have something, he was...well, I don't want to say unscrupulous...I once said to him: "You're here for the SPD." He said: "If the SPD doesn't want me any more, I'll just have to resign."'

Dieter Ertelt wasn't the only one to distance himself from Scholl. The mayor had a growing number of critics and his ideas found less and less favour. His proposal to sell council housing to private investors only just scraped through. The outlet centre under the motorway bridge didn't. Scholl was thwarted, for the first time in his career. Before long, his great dream looked set to be thwarted too, the project that was to bring him immortality in Ludwigsfelde: the naturist thermal spa.

The old swimming baths, where Scholl had worked after his stint at the circus, were to be replaced with new ones. For two years, the mayor had been negotiating with a company that proposed to build an indoor pool with two saunas. The state of Brandenburg had promised funding; it looked as if everything was settled. Then up popped Heinz Steinhart, a new investor, who operated thermal spas and leisure pools all over the country. He took one look at Scholl's swimming-pool plans and said: 'Yes, of course, that's the way everyone plans: a little of everything and nothing proper.'

It was one of those phrases that fired Heinrich Scholl's ambition. Steinhart's proposal might have been twice as expensive as the original one, but the mayor, who always had to be the best, did not want a run-of-the-mill municipal pool in his town; he wanted the best swimming baths in Germany. The thermal spa in Ludwigsfelde was to be his final project: baths worthy of the Romans, the king's parting gift to his people. The only trouble was that his people weren't at all keen on the gift. The town council was up in arms about the twenty-million-euro baths. They wanted a swimming pool, not a wellness temple. The minister of sports, Reiche, refused to subsidise the project.

Steinhart says that when he joined the project 'in the

preliminary stages', he almost backed out again. 'At that time, there were still old Russian barracks where the thermal spa is today. I couldn't imagine bringing leisure to this town.' It was Scholl who convinced him—and it wasn't just the fact that his town had the lowest tax rate in Brandenburg. 'He was a very strong mayor, very shrewd, very well connected. He once told me that he sometimes had to propose the opposite of whatever he wanted to achieve.'

The pool was Heinrich Scholl's new mission. He had been in office for fifteen years and was coming up to retirement, but he fought for the thermal spa as if he had everything to lose. He went to see Steinhart's other baths, met up with architects, learnt the difference between hut saunas and grotto saunas, between hay steam saunas and rose-and-lavender steam saunas. He was always coming up with new ideas. The thermal spa should have an ice cream parlour. It should have a gallery with loungers, so that spa guests who went swimming by moonlight could look up through the glass dome at the stars. The naturist idea was his too. Of course it was.

When the baths were almost finished, Steinhart had said: 'Herr Scholl, we need a selling point for this spa—something that no other pool in the region has.'

'We could do naturism,' Scholl replied.

Steinhart, a Bavarian Catholic, was sceptical to begin with, as were others in town. How were they to organise school swimming lessons in a nudist pool? How were teachers to spend a relaxed Sunday at the spa when they had to live in fear of bumping into one of their pupils with no clothes on? Again, the mayor came up with a solution: two 'swimwear' days a week—Wednesday and Sunday—and the twenty-five-metre pool was to be separate from the nudist area. Heinrich Scholl tried to please everybody. But his opponents were forever finding grounds for criticism. The pressure on Scholl was mounting, and his intestinal trouble was worsening. When he talks about his first years in office, there is no mistaking his pride and surprise at having made it so far. When he talks about the last years, it's all tales of envious people who begrudge him his success.

In his notes, he writes: 'Tougher situation, unpleasant atmosphere, overt accusations—also, alas, from "friends" of my own party. After a great deal of trouble, the spa is completed. It all turns out beautifully—everything high quality, lots of marble, beautiful décor with jewels—but no one can summon up much enthusiasm. On one evening, feeling hopeless, I drink three bottles of red wine with Steinhart!'

For the opening ceremony on Good Friday, the spa was decked out in festive style. Heinrich Scholl and the chair of the town council stood to the ready. At the cash desks, the new cashiers waited for the first guests. Jutta Abromeit, the local reporter, who had followed the construction of the spa with scepticism, was not on the guest list. She came nevertheless and was thrown out by the spa operator. Barred from the premises.

The opening ceremony of the thermal spa was Heinrich Scholl's last moment of glory.

In January 2008 he turned sixty-five and resigned from office. A number of his political fellow-travellers showed up for his farewell party: Klaus Wowereit, Manfred Stolpe, Matthias Platzeck and the social democrats from Lichtenrade. His wife took care of the table décor: she brought along tablecloths and homemade flower arrangements of moss, berries, pinecones and candles. Moss arrangements were Brigitte Scholl's new hobby. She had set up a small workshop in the cellar, and when she took the dog for a walk at midday, she often took a basket with her and left the main path to walk deep into the woods and gather fresh moss.

It was a good party, with several speeches paying tribute to all that Heinrich Scholl had achieved for his town. He enjoyed the evening. For almost twenty years he had been mayor of Ludwigsfelde and it was time for somebody else to take over. It was only right. He looked forward to being able to lie in each morning and not having to go to the town hall every day.

His first day of retirement was just as he had imagined. He slept late, had a long breakfast, opened presents, read cards and letters of farewell, and at midday he went for a walk in the woods with his wife and the dog. After that, still buoyed up by all the speeches about his achievements and merits, he drove back to his office, had coffee with a colleague or two, went over the events of the evening, collected his remaining things and went to bed content.

On the second and third days, he realised that he missed

his appointments, his secretary, his meetings, and lunch in his favourite restaurant, Da Toni's. Scholl's beautiful glass office was now occupied by his former treasurer. This new mayor was a quiet man from the West, who had previously worked in the audit office. One of his first official acts was to have tubs of flowers placed in the big square outside the town hall. Heinrich Scholl was horrified: the tubs ruined the general impression! But nobody seemed to share his annoyance.

For decades, everything Heinrich Scholl did had revolved around his job. His work had given his life rhythm and meaning. His colleagues had also been friends; he could go out for a beer with them in the evenings. Suddenly all that had gone—the work, the rhythm, the friends. He found himself sitting at home at a loose end.

The famous German comedian Loriot once made a film about a couple adjusting to the husband's retirement.

'What are you doing here?' the wife asks at one point.

'I live here,' the man replies.

'But not at this time of day!' the woman says.

Some German cities have counselling services or therapy groups that prepare over-fifties for retirement. They meet regularly to talk about how to cope with the emptiness in their lives. Doctors rate retirement among the most stressful times in a person's life, particularly for men, who never take time out or depart from their rigid routines. The risk of a heart attack increases at retirement age; some men are dead a week after their last day at work.

Brigitte Scholl was two years younger than her husband, and her beauty salon was doing better than ever. She had no plans to stop. Her customers came and went at the house from eight until twelve and from two until six, while her husband sat in the next room reading the paper. Heinrich Scholl could hear his wife talking and laughing. Sometimes she would open the kitchen door and summon him in to greet her customers. 'Heiner, why don't you come and say hello to Frau Weber!'

He decided to look for work again and asked at Daimler whether he could make himself useful at the car works. In consultation with the spa operator, he arranged himself a job on a fee basis: Scholl was to convince the mayors of other towns to have big wellness temples built, like the one in Ludwigsfelde. He had visiting cards printed: *Scholl Consulting—Local and Business Consultancy*.

He set up an office for himself under the roof, where he could work and receive guests. But that proved difficult. He couldn't work when Gitti was in the house. 'Just as I was beginning to get somewhere, I'd have to go downstairs and chop parsley or what have you,' says Heinrich Scholl. What's more, his wife wasn't keen on having people in the house. 'My clients would have had to go upstairs and might have seen into the living room on their way up. Strangers from Daimler sticking their noses into her living room— that wasn't on,' says Scholl.

Heinrich Scholl did not have it easy. Only recently he had been the most powerful man in town, and now he didn't even have a room of his own. His wife ruled that he only use the loo in the cellar and not the one next to her salon. Because of the lady customers.

His health was deteriorating at an alarming rate. Before long, he only weighed sixty-three kilos and was pumped full of drugs—chemotherapy tablets and cortisone. A specialist at the Charité hospital suggested surgery. His doctor in Ludwigsfelde advised against it. The spa operator recommended a clinic on Tenerife where former chancellor Helmut Kohl had gone for treatment. Heinrich Scholl tried everything, even Chinese medicine, but it didn't get any better.

Herbert Walter*, who had worked in the town hall with Heinrich Scholl for many years, says that Scholl often went to see him and his wife at this time. The Walters are one of the oldest families in a village not far from Ludwigsfelde. They have a house with a big garden and a farm with horses, chickens and ducks. Their barn has been converted into holiday apartments and Herbert Walter's wife takes care of the farm and the guests.

It's easy to feel at home, sitting on the Walters' terrace, drinking coffee. They are lovely people and there is always something going on: a friend dropping in, or a neighbour coming by to get flowers or fresh eggs. Heinrich Scholl came to visit almost every other day; he even came when his former colleague was out and only his wife was at home. He took them cake from the baker's or a bottle of wine and told them about his doctors' visits and the difficulties he was having finding an office. He redesigned their garden and helped their son decorate an old worksite trailer that stood in the yard. 'He turned up one day with a straw hat on his head and painted the trailer with little trees and landscapes,' says Ines Walter*.

She and her husband were somewhat surprised that Heinrich Scholl, who had never once been to their house before he retired, was suddenly seeking their company. They were astonished at the loneliness of such a successful, powerful man. Heinrich Scholl even toyed with the thought of moving into one of the holiday apartments on the farm and working from there. But the Walters were uncomfortable at the idea of the former mayor sitting in their barn and were glad when he told them on his next visit that he had found a flat in Berlin's Zehlendorf.

Heinrich Scholl had not actually intended to move properly; he had been looking for an office in Berlin and soon realised that offices are more expensive than flats. But the moment he climbed the stairs and set down his suitcase, he knew that it was the best decision he had made for a long time.

The flat in Zehlendorf was right under the roof and came ready furnished. There was a narrow galley kitchen, an even narrower bedroom and a loft-like living room with sloping walls and a dormer window. Heinrich Scholl bought himself a desk, shelves, a new bed and a Swedish wood-burning stove. He fetched his oil landscapes out of the cellar in Ludwigsfelde and hung them on the walls and he put up two photos on the shelves: a picture of his town-hall mistress as a young woman and another of his favourite actress, Julia Roberts.

It was like back in the days in the circus caravan, only more comfortable. He could sleep as long as he liked, go jogging whenever he felt like it, and eat whenever and whatever he fancied. Nobody nannied him, nobody told him what to wear, nobody wrote him lists. He had told his wife that the flat in Berlin was his office—that it was the best place for him to work and keep up his contacts. If it ever got late, he would stay the night there. Heinrich Scholl says Gitti had agreed.

He attended a computer course at night school, busied himself with his projects for the spa operator, met friends for lunch and began work on a book—an erotic tale. The therapist at Lake Tegern had given him the idea. Heinrich Scholl had told her about the woman in the town hall—how happy he'd been with her and how hard the separation had hit him. 'Write it down,' the therapist said. 'Let it all out.' She had letters or diary entries in mind, but Heinrich Scholl wanted to share his happiness and his great love with others and turned the therapist's assignment into a new project: a book.

When he had written a few pages, he sent them to a former journalist who runs a small self-publishing company. The publisher is an elderly woman with short hair and a gentle whispery voice, who has herself something of a therapist about her. It is generally old people who come to her, wanting to write down their life stories for their children and grandchildren before they die. Scholl, however, a former mayor who wanted to write about his affair, had what was almost a proper idea for a book. 'This woman was the love of his life and he simply never got over it,' says the publisher. 'People who write autobiographies do it for the moments in their lives that meant most to them.'

Heinrich Scholl described how he got to know the woman from the town hall, how he kept walking past her office and leaving her little messages, went out to eat with her, accompanied her to the cinema, or met her at a friend's house. He was very keen on detail, but to be on the safe side, he transposed the action to a business firm and changed the names. Most of it, however, was taken from real life. The publisher embellished the story with lyrical descriptions, quotations from authors and actors, and long dialogues between the main character and a wine-merchant friend. At one point the main character asks the wine merchant whether he's ever contemplated divorce. He replies: 'Divorce, never; murder, yes.'

The publisher wanted the book to be more than a mere report of Heinrich Scholl's experiences; she wanted a proper novel. But Scholl reversed almost all her changes and in the end the final draft scarcely differed from the first. There is no doubt that it bore Heinrich Scholl's signature.

Heinrich Scholl knows no shame and no nuance, and he loves sex scenes. The erotic passages read like assembly instructions for model aeroplanes or IKEA furniture. 'With my right hand I tried to reach her pudenda,' he writes at one point. 'Alas, in vain; my arm was too short.' Heinrich Scholl was more gifted as a technologist than as a writer, but writing not only helped him get over the woman from the town hall; it also filled the seemingly endless days of his retirement. Even the symptoms of his illness gradually vanished. The therapist from the sanatorium seemed to have been right: he needed to write everything down and he needed some time out—that was all.

'I am healthy,' he crows in his notes. 'Meet new people, go a lot to the theatre, opera, cinema. Also have a lot more time for old friends and for enjoyable evenings and conversations. I take up jogging again and go to a gym with a swimming pool in Zehlendorf. Gitti is in charge of the weekends, as usual. I work through my lists, have time to play handball or football, or to go and see friends or to a concert with her. She has become more tolerant.'

In passing, he mentions that a visit or two to a brothel are part of his new life. 'I satisfy my further human needs,' Heinrich Scholl writes, 'in Słubice or sometimes in Artemis. I find it the least complicated way to come by a little affection without entering into dependencies.' Later he scores out 'human' and replaces it with 'male': 'male needs' is the expression he wanted.

Słubice is a Polish border town, Artemis a high-class brothel on Kurfürstendamm. The Polish option was cheaper and Heinrich Scholl preferred it. Word had got about that the new customer had been mayor in Brandenburg. On his first visit there, his Polish counterpart had welcomed him in person and told the brothel manager: 'The best you've got.'

Heinrich Scholl makes his visits to Słubice sound like a celebration of German–Polish friendship. The building is very beautiful: 'like a Mediterranean country estate,' he writes. At the front there is a big wooden carriage entrance, where you can drive your car in. A woman approached him with a smile and led him to a room. 'First I talked to the lady a bit—there again, I'm different from other men. Afterwards you lie there for a while and have a drink and talk. We often went out to eat in a restaurant together. It developed into a wonderful relationship.' If there were such a thing as a visitors' book in a brothel, it might read something like that.

On his next visits, Heinrich Scholl brought coffee for the Polish sex worker and chewing gum for her children. He was playing the West German uncle. 'Whenever I wanted a nice relaxing end to the day, I'd send her a text message, and if she was free, I'd drive over. I was rewarded for my efforts with a great deal of affection. And once I'd left, the story was over. There were no letters, no demands, no "when are you going to ring again?" We can give so much pleasure with so little effort.'

When Heinrich Scholl didn't drive to Poland, he spent his evenings in a club for singles in Steglitz. A beer cost one euro. 'Cheaper than in the supermarket,' says Scholl. There was drinking and dancing. The highlight of the evening was a kind of speed dating, and the rules were always the same. The women sat on one side of the table, the men on the other. They had five minutes to ask each other questions:

'What do you do for a living? Do you have children? What are your hobbies?' Then someone called out 'Change!', the men moved along a chair to the next woman, and it all started over again. At the end, the participants filled in a questionnaire and awarded each other points. The couples with the most points arranged to go on a date.

With his impressive career, his wide range of hobbies and his mountaineering exploits, Heinrich Scholl had excellent prospects with the women of Steglitz. He got to know a Russian woman with two small children and went out to eat with her a few times. But more often than not, he ended up with women his own age who wanted to mother him, introduce him to the family and do his laundry. They reminded him of his wife.

He envied his friend Rainer. Rainer was his age and, like him, had been married to the same woman for decades. But for some time he had also had a Thai girlfriend twenty years younger. The two women knew about each other. It was an open ménage à trois. For almost twenty years, Fischer's wife had had an incurable brain tumour. Her husband nursed her round the clock so that she didn't have to go into a home. His young girlfriend helped him. She had a separate flat, but the three of them spent a lot of time with one another and went on holiday together.

At a birthday party Rainer Fischer attended with his girlfriend, Heinrich Scholl asked him whether she didn't have a friend. Not long afterwards, Fischer said: 'Scholli, I've got something for you.'

Heinrich Scholl first met Nantana Piamsuk* on a winter's day in 2009. She was ten years younger than Fischer's girlfriend, slim with long black hair. The four of them had arranged to have lunch together in Hamlet, a restaurant in Berlin's Charlottenburg. Scholl was the last to arrive and says he nearly lost his nerve and walked out again. 'I get to the restaurant and the three of them are sitting there. Two incredibly pretty little things and Rainer. When I saw my friend alongside them I thought: "You look that old too! Don't kid yourself, Scholl."'

She was called Nantana, but introduced herself as Nani, because that was what her friends called her. Nantana asked whether she could call him Henry; she couldn't pronounce Heinrich. So Heinrich and Nantana became Henry and Nani. She preferred speaking English to German, she said. Luckily, Heinrich Scholl had attended those English classes at the East German adult education centre. What Heinrich Scholl didn't notice was that the beautiful Thai woman preferred not to speak at all.

After lunch, they went for a walk by Lake Schlachten. It was chilly; the women were soon cold. They went into another restaurant. The men put back a lot of red wine; the women drank little.

'It was very enjoyable,' Heinrich Scholl recalls. 'We could talk to each other about anything.'

'He talked and laughed a lot,' says Nantana Piamsuk, 'but it wasn't so funny for me. I didn't laugh. Thais and Germans are different.'

Nantana Piamsuk was twenty-two years old and came from a village in the Mekong region in the east of Thailand. She had two brothers and was the only daughter in the family. A few years before, she had met a south German businessman in Thailand. He promised her a wonderful life, she married him and they moved to Germany together, where they lived in his parents' house. After a few weeks, however, she wanted to get away. She had hoped to do a training course in Germany, find a job and earn some money. Her husband wanted her to stay at home, cook, clean and sleep with him. After eight months, she packed a few belongings and escaped to Berlin.

Andreas Herrmann runs an organisation in Berlin that takes care of Thai women in Germany. It's always the same story, he says: the women have false expectations—and so do the men. 'A holiday in Thailand is one thing; living together is something else again.' The relationships often break down after a few weeks, a result of communication problems and cultural differences. The divorce rate of German–Thai couples is 84 per cent.

Nantana first came to Herrmann's organisation in 2007. She needed a resident's permit. Her marriage wasn't recognised by the German authorities, because she had lived with her husband for less than two years. The organisation helped her. When Heinrich Scholl came along two years later, he took care of the rest. Nantana introduced him to others as 'the mayor'. Sometimes she would talk of her 'German grandad'.

The Thai organisation is on the ground floor of a building in Wedding, formerly one of the poorest parts of Berlin, now starting to become rather fashionable. It was on a six-lane road where trucks hurtle along and planes coming into Tegel airport fly so low you want to duck. But it's cosy nevertheless; the rooms are hung with brightly coloured Thai lamps and in the front garden there's a pergola covered in vines, where barbecues are held in the summer.

Nantana sometimes visited and stayed for an hour while her mayor waited outside in the car. On one occasion, Andreas Herrmann invited Nantana to bring him in. Scholl came in and introduced himself. 'I can't say he was unlikeable,' Herrmann says. 'He asked a lot of questions and inquired about Nantana's problems.'

Heinrich Scholl's new girlfriend had a great many problems: outstanding hospital bills, outstanding rent, gambling debts. Heinrich Scholl paid the lot: her debts, the rent for her flat, a new kitchen, a new corner sofa, a new TV, her mobile phone bills, clothes, handbags, sunglasses, jewellery. Nantana had little money, but high standards. The bags had to be Gucci or Louis Vuitton; the ring that Scholl bought her cost seven hundred euros; the sunglasses four hundred. She had cosmetic surgery to have her eyelids lifted: the mayor paid for that too. In return, she spent time with him, went out to eat with him and slept with him.

For Nantana, the relationship was a deal. For Heinrich Scholl, it was love. He was in his mid-sixties, but this woman made him feel younger than he had ever felt before. She was

not just beautiful; he also found her pleasantly uncomplicated. Unlike the woman from the town hall, she had no
moral qualms, and her demands were more exotic and more
charming than those made by his wife. Gitti wanted him
to trim the hedge and put out the dustbins; Nani wanted
him to shave his pubic hair and buy her expensive presents.
Gitti made him feel like a caretaker; Nani made him feel like
Richard Gere in *Pretty Woman*.

Friends and acquaintances warned him that she was only
exploiting him, but he ignored them.

'After the evening on Lake Schlachten, she gave me her
phone number, and you don't do that unless you're interested,' he says. 'I had that confirmed by a lady friend.' What
he calls the 'bed phase' began five or six weeks later. Nani
had thought his flat was fantastic and been improbably nice
to him—and sensitive. 'She told me that if she'd got to know
someone like me earlier, she'd have had a better picture of
German men. She was glad I was so clean, liked the way I
had a shower twice a day, did sport, took care of myself and
used aftershave. It didn't bother her that I was married.'

Heinrich Scholl was now leading a double life. The week-
days he spent in Berlin with his Thai mistress, but every
Friday evening he made his way to Ludwigsfelde, where he
handed Gitti his bag of dirty laundry and worked through
her list of chores. He was there when she needed him: when
their son visited, when her traditional Christmas brunch in
Potsdam came round, or some other important event they
had to attend as a couple. She insisted on that.

He wanted to be left in peace, and she wanted to show everyone that her world was still intact. That was their arrangement—a ceasefire after forty-six years of marriage.

Friends noticed that Heinrich Scholl was better balanced and more relaxed since moving to Berlin. He raved about his new life and liked asking people round to his flat. The psychologist Joachim Lehmann, spa operator Heinz Steinhart, and even his old acquaintance from early reunification days, Dieter Bartha, were taken to Berlin, where Scholl showed them round his flat as if it were a palace, opening the doors to all the rooms—even to the bathroom, where there was often a black lace bra hanging on the washing line. Like a trophy.

Brigitte Scholl was not allowed in the flat. Heinrich Scholl told his wife he lived life there on his own terms. Sometimes she asked him what he got up to in Berlin. He would reply that he preferred not to talk about it. She didn't persist.

That was the deal. Thus far.

GITTI'S HELPLESSNESS

This time it wasn't a letter but a phone call—a man's voice informing Brigitte Scholl that her husband was betraying her. As before, she'd had her suspicions, and the next time he came home, she confronted him. Heinrich Scholl immediately admitted everything. He said she knew better than anyone how much he needed the affection she'd been denying him for years. He wasn't an old man, after all.

'Yes, you are,' said Gitti. And walked away, leaving him standing there.

It was the same as ever. They didn't shout at each other or slam doors or throw glasses at the walls. When Gitti was sick of her husband, she went to bed. If he didn't work his way through her lists, there was no supper. But these methods no longer got her very far. Her husband had stopped caring whether or not she made supper. He came home to Ludwigsfelde when he felt like it and could drive back to his flat in Berlin at any time, back to his mistress. Brigitte Scholl had lost control. She was powerless.

Never in her life had she felt so helpless, and the worst of it was that no one could be allowed to notice anything.

She confided only in her closest friend, Inge, who lived far removed from Ludwigsfelde. The two women spoke on the phone every morning, and Brigitte Scholl told Inge what she had found out. It was not good news. Not only was her husband's girlfriend thirty years younger than her; she was also a beautician by trade—at least, that's what her husband told her. She probably had her eye on the salon, Brigitte Scholl said to her friend, and announced that, to be on the safe side, she was going to have the house in Ludwigsfelde transferred to her son. The self-confident, energetic Gitti often cried on the phone now and spoke of no longer wanting to live.

Every morning Inge Karther rang Ludwigsfelde to make sure that Gitti hadn't done away with herself. 'She didn't want to carry on,' Inge says. 'She didn't want anything any more, didn't even like leaving the house on her own. She grumbled about Heiner and cursed him, but the next moment she wanted him back. She kept saying you couldn't just throw away all those years.'

Brigitte Scholl asked her friend to ring her husband to tell him what a good wife she was and what a lovely family they had. Inge didn't want to—it was awkward—but she had no choice. The next time Heinrich Scholl was home, Gitti rang Inge. 'Hang on a second, I'll give you Heiner,' she said, and passed the phone to her husband. Her loyal friend in Anklam told Heinrich Scholl that she thought he was treating Gitti shabbily. 'I told him he had no balls. He should have left her five or ten years before, rather than waiting until we were old and nobody wanted us any more.'

Brigitte Scholl's friend Karin Singer was persuaded to drive with her to Berlin to suss out her husband. She still didn't know where he lived. The friends set off, two sixty-five-year-old lady detectives. They soon found the address, but Heinrich Scholl's car was nowhere to be seen; he obviously wasn't in. Karin wanted to leave again immediately, but Gitti had already got out of the car. They walked once round the building, noting that there was no back garden. Apart from that, they saw nothing and nobody. Karin says she was glad when they finally drove off again.

Karin Singer and Inge Karther were part of the small circle of women whom Gitti confided in. Apart from them, the only person she told of her husband's relationship was Helga Gerlich, the social democrat from Lichtenrade. 'Brigitte Scholl rang me up and told me tearfully that Heiner had a girlfriend, because she wasn't enough for him. This woman gave him what she didn't give him. And I said right out: "You must chuck the bloke out! Leave him!"'

That was the advice Brigitte Scholl received from all three friends. It was clear that her marriage was over, that she and her husband no longer had anything in common. But Brigitte Scholl wouldn't leave him for the world. 'She always had this hope that he'd come back. Because he always did come when she needed him,' says Inge Karther. 'They went to see friends together. He turned up punctually and even provided the flowers. She always said to him: "If you hurt me, that's just the way it is, but for other people, we're a couple."'

Brigitte Scholl grew thin; dark rings appeared beneath her eyes. When she opened her salon in the morning, you could tell she'd been crying; it was visible even beneath her make-up. Her customers sensed that something wasn't right, but they seldom inquired; they knew Brigitte Scholl didn't like talking about her worries. One woman, however, risked it—an old woman Brigitte knew from her mother's hair salon.

'What's the matter with you, Frau Scholl?' she asked. 'Is your marriage quite kaput?'

No, no, Brigitte Scholl said quickly. Everything was fine. That evening, the customer's phone rang. It was Heinrich Scholl. He said he was in Ludwigsfelde with his wife and asked her not to spread rumours.

He now had two women and both were a strain on him. One of them wanted his money; the other wanted her marriage back.

Neither of them loved him.

The retired Heinrich Scholl was leading a strenuous life, and it didn't get any easier when he found out that Nani was working in a brothel on the side. At first, he had thought he could rescue her as Richard Gere rescues Julia Roberts in *Pretty Woman*, and tried to initiate his Thai mistress into society. Once he took her to his favourite Italian place in Ludwigsfelde and on another occasion to a friend's birthday party. He drove all over town with her, showing her the town hall and the thermal spa. He even showed her his house, where the unfortunate Gitti was holed up.

'I didn't want to hide any more,' says Heinrich Scholl. 'I'd done that long enough, always showing other people what they wanted to see.'

Nantana Piamsuk went along with everything, as long as Heinrich Scholl satisfied her wishes. Friends and business partners of the once successful mayor followed his transformation in bemusement. Some of them treated him as indulgently as if he was a sick child; others distanced themselves; others again were at a complete loss. His childhood friend, Hans, and Steinhart the spa operator were among those who were given the manuscript of Heinrich Scholl's book to read and shown around his flat in Berlin: kitchen, living room, bedroom, bathroom—and, of course, the black bra.

'The bra was huge,' Steinhart says. 'I thought Scholl was just trying to impress me. As far as I know, Asian women don't have big busts.'

'He was so gone on this woman that he wouldn't see reason,' his friend Hans says. 'Was I supposed to burst his bubble, or what?'

'She fleeced him,' says Rainer Fischer, who had hooked the two of them up.

'She was calculating and devious,' says Andreas Herrmann of the Thai women's support organisation in Berlin.

Nantana Piamsuk took Heinrich Scholl to her native village in Thailand. Her parents met the couple at the airport and drove them to their house, which was larger and better equipped than any of the other huts in the village. Nantana

Piamsuk's family were farming people and owned several fish ponds. At the weekend there was a big wedding ceremony: a festive procession through the village. Heinrich Scholl was the groom, Nantana the bride. The next day, Scholl bought floor tiles for the living room as a present for his hosts. He discovered that the family owed almost their entire wealth to their enterprising daughter. And her German men. Who knows how many bridegrooms had been met at the airport and paraded through the village with Nani? But Heinrich Scholl was not suspicious even now. Back in Berlin, he transferred twenty-five thousand euros to Nani's family in Thailand.

It was supposed to be a loan, but that was soon forgotten. Heinrich Scholl cleared his account, transferred the money to another, and left the statements from the empty account lying around his flat so that Nantana would see he was in the red and pay him back. But her reaction was not the one he had hoped for: she found other men to pay her bills.

Heinrich Scholl began to spy on her. 'He always wanted to know where I was going,' Nantana Piamsuk says. 'He kept tabs on me and followed me. The way he saw it, I had to be with him. He called from a withheld number, or called without speaking. He called and listened and hung up. Constantly. He always knew where I was and who I was with.' Once when a stranger came to her flat, Heinrich Scholl waited on the stairs all night and waylaid the man at dawn.

When the task of surveying his mistress got too much for him, he engaged a private detective agency to record her every move: when she went to work in her massage salon, when she got home, what clothes she was wearing, what men she met. The report the agency gave him is long and absurdly detailed, and uses abbreviations from the world of the secret services. It reads like a Stasi file. Nantana Piamsuk is referred to throughout as the target person, TP. We learn that TP leaves her massage salon at 8.57 pm, takes the U2 underground line towards Pankow-Vinetastrasse, alights at Senefelder Platz, walks towards Schönhauser Allee, enters a REWE supermarket at 9.24 pm and a Thai nightclub at 9.42 pm. In the backyard of the club there is 'evidently a brothel business'.

For hours, the private detectives wait on the pavement outside the club. They observe Scholl's mistress go into the yard towards the brothel at 9.49 pm and return to the club shortly before 10.00 pm. At 12.35 am one of the detectives decides 'to go a step further and find out what TP is doing'. No sooner has he entered the nightclub than he is offered a girl, but it is not 'TP'. Heinrich Scholl's mistress was playing cards with friends, probably for money, and continued to play into the small hours.

It was like a spy film: Brigitte Scholl was snooping on her husband and he was snooping on his mistress. But while Brigitte was managing to keep her life together, Heinrich's was gradually falling apart. His marriage was over, his bank balance had shrunk, and his reputation wasn't looking too good either, after the house in Walther Rathenau Strasse was searched by police. Flight and entertainment bills from

Scholl's time as mayor had been discovered that suggested corruption. Heinrich Scholl was not at home when the investigator rang at the door; his wife was in the middle of treating a customer.

It was the biggest ignominy ever to befall Brigitte Scholl. At least, that's what she thought. Then she was informed in an anonymous letter that her husband's mistress was not a beautician, but a prostitute. It was the final straw. Brigitte Scholl told her friend Inge that she wanted her life back and was going to fight—for the house, not for her marriage. It was over. Brigitte Scholl had hit rock bottom; her husband still had some way to go.

In summer 2011, the spa operators cancelled their fee-based contract with Heinrich Scholl, his most important source of income. Not long afterwards, Nantana Piamsuk split up with him. This time it was for good. On previous occasions he had continued to give her money and presents, and she had come back, only to move out again soon afterwards. He made her final gifts of a laptop and an expensive ring, but it was too late; in October 2011 she packed her bags. She had found a man who lived near Dresden to take care of her. He was Scholl's age—her new German grandad.

SCHOLL'S RETURN

Heinrich Scholl says whenever he started something new in life, he always began by working out how it might end, what opportunities there were, and what risks. The remark is typical of him. In seemingly hopeless situations, he switches onto autopilot. When others lose their heads, he remains cool and unruffled; he can wait without growing impatient and knows when his moment has come. That's how he conquered his wife, acquired his house, became mayor—and it's how he remained mayor for almost twenty years.

He has been known to miscalculate. This has tended to happen when factors came into play that couldn't be calculated by a machine. On such occasions, his life was temporarily thrown out of joint: he gave his notice, broke off whatever he had begun and found himself sitting in the kitchen again, back with his wife.

It happened at the car works and at the circus, and perhaps it also happened in autumn 2011, when Heinrich Scholl suddenly gave up his flat in Berlin and moved back to Ludwigsfelde. He lost control; things didn't run to plan; his system collapsed.

No one understood why Heinrich Scholl wanted to return to his wife in Ludwigsfelde when he had been so happy in Berlin.

Herbert Walter: 'I said to him: "You've got it as good as it gets in Berlin. Don't forget that!"'

Rainer Fischer: '"Are you mad?" I said. "You can't go back home."'

Inge Karther: 'Brigitte told me over the phone that Heiner was planning to move back in with her, bag and baggage. I said: "Well, he's not coming back for love."'

Heike Schramm: 'Nobody knew why he came back. Not even Gitti. She just said: "Imagine, Heike, he's here again with all his boxes. Can you credit it?"'

Karin Singer: 'Suddenly, word was that Heiner was coming back to Gitti. He never gave his reasons, as far as I know.'

Helga Gerlich: 'Brigitte told me cheerfully that Heiner was coming back to her. I told her: "You don't seriously think he's split up with her? Do you believe in Father Christmas? Once a Thai woman, always a Thai woman."'

Horst Karther was one of the last of Heinrich Scholl's acquaintances to be shown round the flat in Berlin. It was in late October, not long before Scholl decided to give up his life in the city. Karther had driven his wife Inge to her class reunion in Ludwigsfelde and was to be taken on a tour of the town by the former mayor while he waited for her. That was Gitti's plan. But Heinrich Scholl wasn't in the mood for Ludwigsfelde and turned off the motorway towards Zehlendorf to show Horst Karther his flat.

This time there was a pair of knickers hanging in the bathroom.

The men had known each other for almost fifty years. They had spent holidays together with their wives and children. The conversation they had on this occasion was unusually frank, at least on Heinrich Scholl's side. He told his holiday mate how happy he was in Berlin, talked to him about the love of his life, Nani, and showed him photos of Thailand. He also mentioned that she cheated on him and how jealous it made him. At the end, however, Heinrich Scholl suddenly announced that it looked as if he'd be moving home.

Horst Karther thought he'd heard wrong. He knew from his wife that Brigitte Scholl wanted to separate from her husband. 'Are you crazy?' he said. 'You don't give up a flat like this, and you know Gitti; you'll have no say in anything if you move back. That's how it was in the past, and now it'll be even worse. She'll gloat if you have to go back.'

Heinrich Scholl said he supposed he'd just have to put up with that, Horst Karther recalls, and he mentioned some shares he'd lost. He'd been badly advised by his bank manager—and his girlfriend was costing him a pretty penny too.

'Why don't you get divorced?' his friend asked.

A divorce was too expensive for Heinrich Scholl. He'd made inquiries of a lawyer: if he and Gitti divorced, he'd have to give her half of his pension.

This corresponds roughly with calculations Heinrich Scholl had made in his diary a few weeks before, later found by the police when they searched the house. 'For the life I'm leading, "our" income isn't enough!' Scholl writes. 'We have 3800 euros together. If, as is looking likely, it comes to divorce, I will have 1800 euros after forty-seven years of marriage. Three years' experience has shown that the business isn't profitable. If anything, contacts and commissions are dropping off. We have no appreciable savings from the past years, which means we're increasingly in the red/burden for me! Reserves exhausted. Endless knock-on effect! I'm the only one who can do anything about it!'

A few days after the class reunion in late October, Frank came to visit his parents in Ludwigsfelde. They got onto the subject of the flat in Berlin; the rent was just under six hundred euros a month. Frank worked out how much money his father had spent on it over the past years: it represented a significant cost. Heinrich Scholl nodded, saying he was planning to give it up and return to Ludwigsfelde to live with his wife. Frank had the impression then that his parents were getting on better with one another.

Heinrich Scholl gave notice of his intention to leave the flat at the end of the year, but moved out a month earlier. His landlady was just as surprised at the precipitate move as everybody else. 'It all happened at such incredible speed,' she says. She knew of Heinrich Scholl's marital trouble and what good it had done him to live in his own flat. 'He said he was a baby getting to know life for the first time—those were his words.' Heinrich Scholl didn't mention his financial straits to the landlady, but told her he was moving back in with his wife because of an operation that might leave him in need of care.

It was not a particularly warm welcome. The unfaithful husband stood outside the house in Ludwigsfelde with his removalist's boxes. When Brigitte Scholl saw the boxes, she told him he could take half of them away again immediately. Scholl's things were loaded back into the car and driven to his friend Herbert's barn. The rest he deposited in the converted cellar of their house, where he and his wife had once danced with his social democrat friends from Lichtenrade.

It seemed a lifetime ago. There hadn't been a fire in the fireplace for years. The cellar was used for washing and ironing; Heinrich Scholl had his painting workshop down there, and Brigitte Scholl a small room where she kept the equipment for her moss arrangements. Otherwise it was a place for storing things that were only rarely used: Heinrich Scholl's mountaineering gear, his football boots, the Christmas and Easter decorations, toys for the grandchildren, and all those little things you don't throw out because they might come in useful at some point—among them, Gitti's sunhats, and shoelaces from Heinrich Scholl's old trainers. Everything was neatly hung up or packed in cardboard boxes and labelled. Brigitte Scholl was a fastidious woman; everything in her house had to be neat and tidy and in its place. She employed two cleaning women: one for the house and one for the cellar. The cleaners were not allowed to move the furniture, and for reasons of hygiene they were not to pour the cleaning water down the loo, but had to empty it into the gutter outside the house.

It was also for reasons of hygiene that her husband had to use the bathroom in the cellar after moving back, rather than the one next to her salon. It would be best if he slept down there too, in among all his files. The files drove Brigitte Scholl up the wall. She decided to ask one of her customers, an accountant, to go through her husband's stuff and throw away what was no longer needed. She asked her friend Inge whether she didn't have any use for Heiner's books.

It was just as Horst Karther had predicted. Brigitte Scholl let her husband move home, but she gloated over his defeat and made him suffer more than ever. It is hard to say what his reaction was. The days and weeks after Heinrich Scholl's return from Berlin are something of a mystery.

He was as busy as ever, attending to a Chinese delegation interested in developing business parks, setting up a planning office for the company that was to expand the thermal spa, and stepping into the breach when a reader cancelled shortly before the traditional Christmas reading at the municipal library. At the end of the reading, he wished his audience a merry Christmas—from him and his wife.

Heinrich Scholl says it was a good time, even at home; his wife had become more tolerant and gave him more freedom than before. But Brigitte Scholl told her friend Inge that her husband had grown more strong-willed and taken to answering her back. When she said, 'Heiner, fetch this, fetch that,' he'd stand his ground and hurl abuse at her, Inge says.

The police found emails to Nantana dating from this time on Scholl's computer. He writes how much he misses her and begs her to ring him. 'Why don't you ring? Please ring me—I'd like to hear your voice, at least. Kisses, Henry.' On 31 October, one of the days when Heinrich Scholl was clearing out his flat in Zehlendorf, Nantana's Berlin flat was burgled. The thief let himself in with a key and stole almost exclusively gifts from Heinrich Scholl, mainly expensive handbags. Heinrich Scholl denies burgling his mistress. 'That's rubbish,' he says. 'I wouldn't risk it in broad daylight. Why on earth would I fetch the bags back?'

Nantana Piamsuk, however, suspects him. It scared her, she says; she moved to Saxony, in south-east Germany, to live with her new man, but told Scholl she was in west Germany. When he discovered the truth, she booked a flight to Thailand and left in early December.

She was fleeing Heinrich Scholl. But she couldn't shake him off.

Scholl texted Nantana Piamsuk relentlessly, telling her he wanted to visit her, or claiming he was already in Thailand. She deleted his messages without reading them. She entered a convent and had her hair shaved off. Someone attempted to break into her new boyfriend's flat back in Germany. The man received a threatening letter assembled from newspaper fragments: 'If only you'd left the tart in the brothel. Now your wife's turning in her grave a second time.'

The author of the letter couldn't be traced. Scholl says he had nothing to do with either the burglary or the letter, but the police later found an entry in his diary from 6 December. The address of Nantana Piamsuk's new boyfriend had been noted down and crossed out. The same address had also been entered into Scholl's sat nav. The police also searched his computer, looking through his files and browser history, and discovered the name of Nantana Piamsuk's new lover three-hundred-and-twenty-five times—that and a copy of the obituary notice the man had issued after his wife's death six months before.

Heinrich Scholl, coolly calculating technologist, far-sighted mayor and model husband, seemed to have vanished. He later said he hadn't wanted to lose touch with Nani and wanted to get his money back, but he acted as if the ground had opened up beneath him.

While his mistress was on another continent, Scholl sat at home in Ludwigsfelde, feverishly rewriting his love story. He had been working on the manuscript for years, continually updating it. The love story of a businessman with marital problems had given way to a kind of erotic novel in which Heinrich Scholl had rewrought his brothel visits with fond attention to detail. Henry, the hero was called, sharing the author's pseudonym. Henry Sanders was a tireless lover, a Casanova. Now the book was to be published at last—by Christmas at the latest, Scholl told his publisher. At the eleventh hour he changed the name of Henry's mistress from Tanja to Lydia, because a friend had thought Tanja too Russian-sounding.

He collected the first two hundred and fifty copies from

the small private publisher and gave them to friends and acquaintances as Christmas presents. His friend Herbert got one, his friend Hans, the vet and his wife, the spa operator and the building contractor from Grossbeeren. Rainer Fischer was given two copies—one for him and one for his daughter, who worked for an academic publishing house. Scholl seemed to be hoping for a literary breakthrough—or else he wanted to propagate a version of his life he could live with. It was a portrait of a man in full possession of his faculties—yet in real life, the people around him were starting to wonder if Heinrich Scholl might in fact be losing the plot.

He took the remaining books to Berlin to flog at a Christmas market. Heinrich Scholl, once the most successful mayor in East Germany, a co-founder of social democracy in Brandenburg and a conqueror of the world's highest peaks, wandered from stall to stall with his box of books, hawking his erotic love story. The stall holders shook their heads. No one in Berlin knew the little man. Scholl left his box at the entrance to the market, on the ground.

He didn't mention the book to his wife, but he didn't hide it either. He left it in the desk in his study, to which she had access at all times. Once she caught him reading it and asked what it was. Heinrich Scholl said a friend of his had written the book; he was proofreading it.

'Just imagine, he's proofreading a sex book now. What a chump!' she said to her friend Karin. Over the phone to her schoolmate, Joachim Lehmann, she said that her husband was busy with 'some pornographic stuff'.

Her husband was more and more of a stranger to her.

Heinrich Scholl told her of a contract in China and announced that he would soon be away again for a few months. Brigitte Scholl didn't seem to mind. She told one of her cleaning ladies that her husband would soon be going abroad—then order would return at last.

Local reporter Jutta Abromeit met Heinrich Scholl shortly before Christmas at a charity event at the town hall. He was completely relaxed, she says. He looked as if he were planning something—something big that he couldn't talk about.

At the Advent market in a neighbouring village, many people from Ludwigsfelde saw the former mayor and his wife together for the last time. Brigitte Scholl was accompanied by a girlfriend; Heinrich Scholl was selling bratwurst with his friend Herbert. The royal couple of Ludwigsfelde were united—something nobody had seen for a long time.

Brigitte Scholl seemed to be relishing it. When asked by a customer what her husband was doing there, she replied: 'Heiner's come back to me.'

GITTI'S SECRET

When her mother drank herself to death, Brigitte Scholl told everyone she had fallen down the stairs. An accident. When her sister died shortly afterwards, the explanation was again 'a fall, an accident', this time in the bathroom. These were variations on reality that Brigitte Scholl could live with— stories she could entrust to the people of Ludwigsfelde.

A few months before her death, she herself fell down the stairs.

She had a bruise above her eye and a deep gash on her forehead. It was a curious injury for a fall downstairs and looked more as if someone had hit her in the face with a sharp object, but Brigitte Scholl insisted it was an accident. She did, however, put about different versions of the incident.

Heinrich Scholl says Gitti told him she had slipped on her way out of the bathroom and crashed into the shoe cupboard. Friends were told she had fallen down the cellar stairs. Customers heard that she'd fallen in the bathroom.

Did she combine the lie about her mother's death with the one about her sister's death?

Siegfried Schmidt, a school friend, saw quite a lot of

Brigitte in the months leading up to her death, because they organised the class reunion together. On one occasion, she had looked puffy, as if she'd been crying. When he asked what was wrong, she said she'd just been to the dentist. Root canal treatment. The next time he saw her, she had a bruise on her head. She gave him the story about falling downstairs. Siegfried Schmidt said: 'Let me have a look at your arms and legs then. After a fall downstairs they must be black and blue.' Brigitte Scholl swiftly changed the subject.

She acted strangely in the days and weeks leading up to her death. Often it was little things that only assumed significance after her death. Brigitte Scholl's cleaning woman was told in passing about the arrangements she had made for her funeral. Everything was settled, Brigitte said. A grave just for her; she'd even chosen the plot and the funeral music. The cleaning lady was taken aback by this unexpected disclosure. Brigitte Scholl had never confided in her about private matters.

When her son visited for the last time in late October, Brigitte Scholl had shown him a shoebox containing envelopes of money—five thousand euros altogether. She told Frank that if anything should happen to her, he should take the money for himself; his dad didn't know about it.

Frank didn't ask his mother whether she was ill or what had given her the idea that something might happen to her. Ever since his childhood, he had carried out his mother's instructions without comment. If these were calls for help, they were barely audible—but Brigitte Scholl had never asked anyone for help, and perhaps this was as close as she could come.

On 27 December, her school friend Maria Zucker called in at Rathenau Strasse. Maria's husband had been seriously ill for a long time and Brigitte Scholl wanted to take her mind off things. She showed her the Christmas tree, offered her coffee and promised to drop in some time in the next few days with fresh moss for winter arrangements in her window boxes. Maria didn't even sit down; she had to get back to her husband in hospital. But Brigitte Scholl came up with one more thing: a poem that her friend simply had to hear.

'Heiner, go and fetch the poem about the little candle from upstairs,' she said to her husband in the Brigitte Scholl tone that brooked no argument. Heinrich Scholl was in his armchair, reading the paper. 'It can wait,' Maria demurred. But Brigitte Scholl wouldn't rest until her husband had got up and gone upstairs. When he returned, he had a slip of paper in his hand and read Maria a poem. It was about a little candle whose clear light brings people joy and warms their hearts. The candle itself grows smaller and smaller until it eventually goes out, but it leaves behind it only joy, not sorrow.

It was one of those calendar quotes that Brigitte Scholl was fond of distributing to friends and acquaintances. Maria wasn't listening properly and would probably have forgotten all about the poem if it hadn't been the last time she saw her friend. Two days later, Brigitte Scholl was dead, buried in the woods under a blanket of moss. To this day, Maria wonders whether the poem was supposed to herald her death. The dying candle, Brigitte, the moss. She had wanted to gather her some.

Everyone tries to make sense of a tragedy.

Now, in retrospect, there are other things that seem strange too. One neighbour remembers meeting Brigitte Scholl on the street and being wished a peaceful New Year. Peaceful! She'd never said that before, the neighbour says. A customer wondered why Frau Scholl had told her at her last two beauty appointments where she could order her skin cream. Usually Brigitte Scholl got hold of the cream herself and you bought it from her in the salon. She had suddenly begun to talk of closing her beauty studio and started to try out other salons between Christmas and New Year so as to be able to recommend one to her customers. But her calendar was full of appointments until well into March.

Brigitte Scholl last spoke to her friend Inge on 27 December. It was a long phone call. They told each other how they had spent Christmas. The Scholls had planned to go to Frank's, but had cancelled because of Ursus. The long journey was too much of a strain on the old dog. Brigitte Scholl said she and Heiner had been to hear the traditional fanfare from the tower of the town hall, and to friends in Potsdam for brunch. At the end of the conversation, she said there was something else she absolutely had to tell her friend, but it would have to wait; Heiner was there. She'd ring again later.

Inge Karther never found out what it was Brigitte Scholl wanted to tell her. The next time she rang her friend, Frank answered.

He said: 'Mum's dead and Dad's being questioned.'

BENEATH THE MOSS

On 30 December at 2.51 pm, a phone call came in to Ludwigsfelde police station. A man was on the phone. His name was Scholl. He was calling from the woods and said it looked as if his missing wife had been found. The doctor on call and the local police were the first on the scene. They were met by three men in all-weather jackets, sturdy footwear and woolly hats: Heinrich Scholl, his son, Frank, and their family friend, the local vet, Werner Singer.

The Scholls' son was standing by the road to give directions. Heinrich Scholl and the vet were waiting in the woods. Frank was crying, Heinrich Scholl pale and trembling. The vet led the way to the spot where they had found the ladies' shoes. Standing by the shoes, you could just make out the two moss-covered mounds in the afternoon dusk. The larger mound was the length of a person; two feet stuck out at the bottom and on one side a hand was visible. The other mound was smaller and rounder. The scene resembled a burial site, a ritual burial site. Fairy graves. When the policemen later had to describe finding Brigitte Scholl and her dog, they used the word 'funeral-like'.

More and more emergency services arrived: the criminal investigation department, the fire brigade, forensics. A large area was cordoned off and floodlights were set up. When the state police forensic experts from Potsdam started work, it was already dark. On the police video, five figures in white suits and blue shoes can be seen removing pads of moss, twigs and leaves from a mound and packing them in plastic bags. Handful after handful of moss and leaves. They work slowly until the uniform musty grey of the moss begins to give way to other colours: the dark blue of a jacket, the yellow of a rubber glove, the white of a woman's skin.

At first, everything seemed to point to a sex crime. The dead woman was lying on her back, her head in a plastic bag, her trousers pulled down, her knickers hanging around her left leg. A condom and a Viagra pill were found in Brigitte Scholl's pocket. At the autopsy, however, the forensic experts discovered that the rape had been faked. There was no evidence of sexual intercourse, but there was bruising on the chin, wrists and upper arms, and strangle marks on the neck. They concluded that Brigitte Scholl had been punched in the face and fallen backwards. Then the killer had knelt down, put a shoelace round her neck and pulled it tight. Finally he had placed the plastic bag over her head, pulled down her trousers and knickers and deposited the Viagra pill and the condom in her pocket.

The shoelace round Brigitte Scholl's neck had been knotted twice at the front. During her death throes, the killer must have been looking his victim right in the eye.

The dog had been killed in the same way. Strangled. It is the hardest way to kill an animal. A dog has a stronger neck than a human. The killer had twisted a stick into the shoelace, like a tommy bar. Over the dog's muzzle was a fruit-gum bag, tied up with a length of washing line. Brigitte Scholl had liked fruit gums. No evidence of resistance or struggle was found. In fact hardly any evidence was found at all: no footprints, no fibres, no signs of dragging. The police assumed that the victim had been caught unawares while walking her dog in the woods. The yellow rubber glove on Brigitte Scholl's hand was to protect her from the caterpillars of the oak processionary moth, which is common in the forests of Brandenburg and can trigger dangerous skin reactions.

Ricarda Hoss* was the first detective to arrive at the crime scene. She asked Heinrich Scholl to sit in her squad car and answer a few routine questions. But Heinrich Scholl didn't need questions to make him talk. The detective still clearly recalls how the stranger in the woods told her about his semi-detached house in Ludwigsfelde where he lived with his wife—although until recently he had rented a small flat in Berlin. A psychologist at Lake Tegern had advised him to take this step, because he had been seriously ill. Fifty per cent of his illness had to do with his stressful job as mayor; thirty-five per cent with his wife. His wife was very domineering. She hadn't let him hang up his pictures; it had made him happy to nail a picture on the wall of his own flat at last. He had once planted early bloomers in the garden and his wife dug them all up again.

Ricarda Hoss had been working for the criminal investigation department for twenty years and during that time had questioned many relatives of murder victims. She expected Heinrich Scholl to tell her about the hell he'd gone through since his wife's disappearance. Instead, he talked about his early bloomers and how his wife had oppressed him. It had almost the ring of a confession.

When the detective asked him how he had spent the day, he fell quiet. The dead woman's husband seemed suddenly tired; he put his hand to his forehead and closed his eyes. Questioning was suspended.

The operation in the woods went on for over five hours. There were still figures walking about in white plastic suits when Heinrich and Frank Scholl and the vet were given permission to leave. The vet's pick-up truck was parked on Siethener Strasse, where they had left it that afternoon when they set off to look for Brigitte Scholl. They drove back through town. It was dark and quiet in Ludwigsfelde. The second-to-last day of the year. They had planned to celebrate New Year's Eve together. Brigitte Scholl had invited the vet and the psychologist with their wives. Three couples, like in the old days. They were going to sit by the fire, listen to music, maybe dance. Brigitte Scholl had been looking forward to the evening.

Karin Singer, the vet's wife, was standing at her front door with a tear-stained face. She took Frank and Heinrich Scholl in her arms, led them into the house, poured tea and handed round little sandwiches she had prepared in the hours of waiting.

The four of them sat in the living room where Brigitte Scholl had sat so often. Everything was just the same as the day before when she had rung for the last time to talk about New Year's Eve. The Christmas tree lights were on; there was ski jumping on TV. You could imagine the phone ringing at any moment and it would be Brigitte Scholl telling her friend what to bring to the party.

The telephone remained silent; nobody touched the sandwiches or made conversation. Karin Singer asked the odd question:

'Was it really Gitti?'

'What happened?'

'Where was the dog?'

'What do the police say?'

Frank sobbed. Heinrich Scholl stared into space. They didn't look at each other; they didn't speak to each other. Only two sentences stuck in Karin Singer's head:

Heinrich Scholl: 'Now I've got this on my plate too.'

Frank Scholl: 'Well, if that's your only worry...'

Frank spent the next week in Ludwigsfelde. He had decided to keep his father company until it was clear what had happened to his mother. His father, however, didn't seem to care whether he had company or not. On the first night, Heinrich Scholl moved back into the bedroom his wife had banished him from. When Frank asked him a question, he would say 'Yes' or 'No'. Nothing else. Sometimes he would step outside the door for a smoke. In the evenings, he lit candles and drank red wine. Most of the time he sat at the table going through documents.

'What on earth are you doing?' his son asked.

'The tax return,' Heinrich Scholl replied.

They had always had a good relationship. When Frank was little, Heinrich Scholl had made things with him. When Frank went to school, Heinrich Scholl was on the parents' committee and helped him with his homework. During Frank's apprenticeship, he persuaded him to study for his school-leaving exams at evening school, and waited at a crossroads every day to hand him his supper. When Frank wanted to emigrate to the West, he drove him to the reception centre. When Frank moved into his first flat, he helped him do it up.

Heinrich Scholl was always there when Frank needed him. When Frank turned forty, he had thanked his father for all the support he had given him over the years. Heinrich Scholl says he cried, he was so touched.

Now Frank thought his father was acting strangely. His wife was dead, but he carried on living his life as if she had only gone on holiday for a couple of weeks. The news that Brigitte Scholl had already made arrangements for her funeral and wanted to be buried alone, without him, he received with apparent indifference. His mind seemed to be on other things. He told Frank that the thermal spa in Ludwigsfelde was being expanded and that he was to help. He also spoke of the new project in China.

'What do you want in China at your age?' his son asked.

Heinrich Scholl told a friend about transformers that could be used to operate street lamps on the Crimean Peninsula. Great place to live, too, the Black Sea, he said; a German pension was worth something down there.

He informed his publisher that he'd like a second edition of his book; there were various spelling mistakes, and besides, the name of Henry's mistress hadn't been changed consistently: in some places it still said 'Tanja' rather than 'Lydia'. For a while they discussed whether or not 'Tanja' sounded Russian. Then, shortly before hanging up, Heinrich Scholl mentioned that his wife was dead.

On 31 December, at half past nine on the dot, Joachim Lehmann and his wife stood on the doorstep of the house in Rathenau Strasse in evening dress, bearing sparkling wine, doughnuts and small presents. They had come to celebrate New Year with Gitti and Heiner and the vet and his wife, as arranged. The Lehmanns lived in a nearby village; the news of Gitti's death hadn't yet reached them, and Heinrich Scholl hadn't cancelled. The house was dark when they rang the bell. Frank came to the door and said: 'Nothing doing here.'

Journalists had found out that the dead woman in the woods was the former mayor's wife, but not how she had died. The police issued no information, so as not to influence the investigations. Every day a new, creepier rumour about the murder swept through the small town. First the Russian mafia were behind it, then the Thai mafia; a few days later it was the Polish cigarette mafia. Frank's biological father got in touch with his son and asked whether it was true that Gitti had been killed with a shotgun. One of the Scholls' cleaners had seen a jogger the day before the murder who struck her as suspicious, because he wasn't sweating. An Asian, she said. An Asian who didn't sweat. Other people in Ludwigsfelde reported that the victim had been so badly disfigured by fireworks that it had taken DNA tests to identify her. An anonymous caller warned police that the murderer was already looking for his next victim.

Brigitte Scholl's customers also received a call. It was their former mayor telling them that, owing to his wife's death, he had to cancel all their appointments. It had been Frank's idea. He wanted to prevent unsuspecting elderly ladies from turning up at the house in Rathenau Strasse at eight in the morning for their beauty appointments. Frank read out the phone numbers. His father made the calls. Most of the customers were so shocked they didn't even offer their condolences.

It was one of the last joint endeavours of father and son.

On New Year's Day they drove to Potsdam together to have lunch in a restaurant. On their way back, they passed the woods where Brigitte Scholl had been murdered. Heinrich Scholl suggested stopping. Frank didn't want to. Heinrich Scholl got out alone and walked into the woods. His son saw him bend down. Later he drove back to the spot alone to see whether his father had hidden anything there. He found nothing. Frank called the criminal investigations department and said his father was acting suspiciously.

The police were not surprised. The call for witnesses had drawn responses from people who had seen Scholl at the edge of the woods with his wife and the dog on 29 December, although when questioned by the police, he had said he hadn't accompanied her on her walk that day, but had been busy with surveying work at the spa. Neither the construction firm nor the swimming pool operators could confirm having asked him to carry out surveying work. Heinrich Scholl had only been seen at the spa until twelve o'clock and had turned up to his one o'clock lunch with his business friend in Berlin over an hour late. For the time of the murder, between twelve and one o'clock, he had no alibi.

Brigitte Scholl's Mercedes was found in a side street near the station; the key was in a heap of leaves. Two witnesses had seen a man driving through town in her car. Neither of them had recognised the former mayor, but the police assumed nevertheless that it could only have been Heinrich Scholl: he had strangled his wife, abandoned the car near the station and driven to Berlin in his Nissan, which he had left parked outside the spa. Later that afternoon, he had played the concerned husband for neighbours, friends and acquaintances; the next day he had organised the search for his wife and led his son and the vet unawares to the crime scene. Heinrich Scholl had wanted to be there when his wife's body was found, so as to leave footprints and DNA.

The motive, too, soon seemed clear: the wrecked marriage. The police knew about the Thai mistress; Heinrich Scholl's text messages to her had been found on his phone.

A witness told them of Scholl's autobiographical sex novel.

Two weeks after the crime, an application was submitted to the public prosecutor's office in Potsdam for permission to issue a warrant for Heinrich Scholl's arrest.

Scholl knew nothing of this, but he sensed that he was being circled. He had been questioned repeatedly by the police; on one occasion the questioning had gone on for six hours and had felt like an interrogation. He told acquaintances he was the police's main suspect. When Heike Schramm took him lunch one day, she found him sitting in the dark with the funeral guest list, 'small and terribly sad, like a little gnome', she says. When Joachim Lehmann went to visit, Scholl was sitting in the kitchen by candlelight. He offered his guest lukewarm tea and seemed depressed and abstracted. It was only when he got onto the subject of his book—his love story—that Heinrich Scholl came to life again. He gave Joachim Lehmann a copy and told him how he had designed the cover with real rose petals.

His old friend Hans Streck drove to the Egyptian Museum in Berlin with Scholl. It was Heinrich Scholl's idea; he wanted to get out of Ludwigsfelde. He wandered through the rooms like a tourist, admiring the layout of the museum and the beauty of Nefertiti. Later, over dinner in a restaurant, he began to cry and was almost impossible to pacify. Hans Streck had known his friend since he was twelve. He had never seen him cry before.

A few days later, Heinrich Scholl had a car accident. He was on his way to Dresden to look up an old friend he and

Gitti had once spent holidays with on the Baltic. It wasn't clear why he wanted to see this friend rather than anyone else; it seemed to be another of the traumatised widower's strange whims. Near Cottbus, Heinrich Scholl drove into a truck. His Nissan was a write-off; he escaped with bruising. He swore it had been an accident: the truck had switched lanes without indicating. But the truck driver told the police he *had* indicated, and when Brigitte Scholl's friend Inge later asked Heinrich Scholl how he was coping by himself, he said: 'I'm sorry. I regret it. Almost brought it off on the motorway.'

The funeral went smoothly. There was no scandal, no argument, nobody broke down. Everything was as Brigitte Scholl had planned. In the chapel was a big picture of her with Ursus in her arms. Frank gave the eulogy. He spoke of his mother's popularity in the town, of her dedication to others. Only her closest friends came: Inge Karther, Karin Singer and their husbands, Joachim Lehmann and his wife, their social democrat friends from Lichtenrade and Gitti's school friend Maria. They took up their wreaths and followed the undertaker. At the head of the funeral procession was Heinrich Scholl with a wreath of white roses.

Ludwigsfelde's cemetery is a park-like enclosure with a chapel, tall trees and old family tombs; it is one of the few places where the town loses its cold, desolate character. Even the constant roar of the motorway seems a little quieter. The townspeople like coming here to meet acquaintances or walk their dogs. The cemetery is busier than the square in front of the town hall. Only right at the back on the left is there a deserted spot, where no candles burn and people seldom pass. There is a small urn plot here: number 146. This is Brigitte Scholl's grave.

Later, in the restaurant, Heinrich Scholl went from table to table. He looked in a bad way, says Horst Karther, who offered to visit him in Ludwigsfelde. 'If you're in trouble, Heiner, I'll come.' Heiner replied: 'Oh, give over, I'd rather come to you.' They talked for a while, among other things, about Gitti. Scholl was surprised at how fondly the mourners spoke of his wife. At the end he said: 'Gitti loved everyone—just not me.'

Two days after the funeral, at dawn, the police turned up at Heinrich Scholl's house. He was still in his pyjamas when he opened the door. In the hall, the public prosecutor read him the arrest warrant: he was under strong suspicion of the heinous murder of Brigitte Scholl. And the dog. Scholl was allowed to get dressed; then he had to hand over his keys and phone. In the car, handcuffs were put on him. He asked for permission to ring his son.

Shortly before ten, Frank's phone rang. He had returned home to Wiesbaden, five hundred kilometres away. The chief superintendent informed him that his father had been arrested early that morning and was currently being held for questioning by the homicide squad in Potsdam.

THE TRIAL

Ten months later, at 9 am on 18 October 2012, the hearing against Heinrich Scholl was opened in the Potsdam Criminal Court. He was charged with 'the heinous murder of a human being in coincidence with the killing of a vertebrate animal without reasonable cause'.

News broadcasters from Berlin and Brandenburg were there to announce the start of the trial. The first visitors were outside the court at half past seven. Among the first in the queue were an old teacher of Heinrich Scholl, a chiropodist who had been a member of the district assembly alongside the defendant twenty years before, friends, and townspeople who couldn't believe that their former mayor was accused of murder.

No one could believe it. Since being arrested, Heinrich Scholl had maintained that he had nothing to do with his wife's murder. When friends visited him in custody, he turned his hands palm up and asked: 'Can these hands kill?'

He had hired two prestigious lawyers, Stefan König and Heide Sandkuhl. König is known for defending criminal politicians such as the former Stasi boss Erich Mielke. Heide

Sandkuhl, who was based in Potsdam, had defended plenty of Brandenburg politicians against charges of corruption or criminal behaviour while in office.

While his lawyers prepared his case, Heinrich Scholl had by no means been idle himself. The arrest warrant stated that he was lacking an alibi for the time of the murder. He had, however, been sighted by witnesses near the woods. With his wife. When the vet went to see him in prison, Scholl asked him to track down some horse riders who had seen him and Gitti in the woods on 28 December, the day before the murder; he wanted to prove that the witnesses must have got the day wrong.

He also placed a notice in a weekly paper that was delivered free to all households in Ludwigsfelde. The notice read:

> Dear residents of Ludwigsfelde, spa guests, visitors to the town,
>
> As you will be aware from radio and television, I, Heinrich Scholl, am suspected of having killed my wife and our dog. In consequence, I have been in custody since 25 January 2012.
>
> I would like to ask you for your help! Did anyone see me in or around the thermal spa between 12 am and 1 pm on 29 December? I was wearing a three-quarter-length dark blue all-weather jacket and blue jeans.

The letter appeared on page six under the rubric 'Law and Order', usually the reserve of solicitors' ads. It caused a stir throughout the country. No one could remember a defendant ever daring to use a small ad to find defence witnesses from prison, but it was not against the law. In Ludwigsfelde, people wondered whether Heinrich Scholl had finally gone completely mad, or whether he really was innocent. The case was growing more and more bizarre. At the end of the letter, Heinrich Scholl thanked his readers for their attention as he had once thanked them for voting for him. Beside the notice was a photo: Heinrich Scholl in collar and tie, the illustrious mayor everybody knew. He was smiling wearily.

The man who entered Courtroom 8 in Potsdam Criminal Court at nine o'clock was not smiling. Heinrich Scholl wore a blue polo shirt under an open jacket and was flanked by two uniformed guards. His hair was shorter than usual. He stared at the floor. When the flurry of flashes ended and the photographers were ushered out, he glanced up and nodded at local reporter Jutta Abromeit and at a friend in the gallery. He did not look at his son.

Frank was sitting opposite on the side of the prosecution, a heavy man with the bewildered look of a child. His face was red, his forehead beaded with sweat.

Until August, Frank had visited his father in prison. Heinrich Scholl had protested his innocence to his son, as to all his visitors, but Frank didn't know whether he could believe him. He didn't know anything. He was the suspect's son; the police told him nothing. Both the public prosecution and Scholl's lawyers denied him access to their files. The start of the trial was repeatedly delayed. Frank sat at home in Wiesbaden, trying to figure out what had happened. He was getting nowhere alone. In the summer he hired a lawyer and decided to appear at the hearing as a co-plaintiff. Now the court had to put the results of the investigation at his disposal.

The files seemed to yield a clear picture: Heinrich Scholl had no alibi for the time of the murder, his mobile phone signal indicated that he had been near the crime scene, forensics had found traces of his DNA on the shoelace and on the deceased woman's underwear, and the prosecution had minutely reconstructed the events of that day with the help of witness statements. There were, however, doubts as to whether it would be possible to prove in court that Heinrich Scholl had murdered his wife. The DNA traces and mobile phone records were not unequivocal proof of culpability. Furthermore, there were neither eyewitnesses nor a confession.

Heinrich Scholl, who had always been a big speaker in his politician days, had decided to exercise his right to silence in court. He spoke only one word, when he was asked whether his date of birth and other biographical data were correct: 'Yes.' Her client needed a little time to acclimatise, Heide Sandkuhl explained. Sitting upright, he stared at his hands, his lips pressed so tightly together they were almost blue. This time it wasn't the most beautiful woman at stake, the best Mardi Gras costume, the next election victory, or conquering Everest: this time, everything was at stake.

In Germany, criminal offences are tried by a judge, or panel of judges, not by a jury. Serious offences such as murder are heard by a panel of two or three professional judges and two 'lay judges', who are members of the community nominated to serve on the court. The presiding judge orchestrates the trial, deciding what order the evidence will be presented in and questioning witnesses and the defendant directly. Presiding over Scholl's case was Judge Tiemann, a slightly built, softly spoken man who sat enthroned between the associate and lay judges like a headmaster.

The first witnesses Tiemann called were the police who had spoken to Heinrich Scholl the day his wife had disappeared. Neighbours and friends followed—everyone who had seen Heinrich Scholl during those December days, or could comment in any way on his problems and his marriage. Half the town was on the witness list, along with many others: son, vet, cleaning women, beautician, Berlin landlady, the victim's best friends, the doctor on call, the head of investigations, the publisher, the former mistress, a driving instructor, a tax advisor, SPD friends, a florist, a former lover of the deceased, the Macedonian landlord from Heinrich Scholl's favourite Italian restaurant, the cashier from the naturist spa, the spa operator, business friends. As if performing on stage, they made their entrances in Potsdam Criminal Court and then exited again. Scholl sat there throughout it all, furiously taking notes.

'Atypical' was the word used by the policeman on duty at Ludwigsfelde police station on 29 December to describe Heinrich Scholl's behaviour. He had wondered why anyone would go to the police after only four hours just because his wife hadn't come home. Scholl's neighbour described how the former mayor had rung at her door that same evening and flung his arms around her neck in tears. She had known him for years, was aware that he'd hardly been with his wife lately, and was surprised at the tears. Never before, she said, had she seen him so emotional. Other witnesses also reported that Heinrich Scholl had acted differently that day, more conspicuously somehow, even in the morning, when his wife was still alive. Instead of walking past the cashier at the thermal spa as he usually did, he called out: 'Gosh, it's busy in here!' He apologised for stopping in a no-parking area to a woman having a cigarette break outside the spa: 'Just got to pop in quickly, then I'll be off.' At the bank he had trouble withdrawing cash and walked back and forth in front of the security cameras several times. In Hamlet, the Berlin restaurant where he had lunch with his friend, the waitress clearly remembered him because he'd left such a big tip.

The vet described how 'Heiner' had rung at his door and told him his wife was gone. The next day they'd gone in search of her together with Heiner's son. It had been Frank who'd discovered the shoes. 'They were standing there as if on display,' the vet said. Not far from the shoes, he himself had then seen 'something covered, in the shape of a body' and 'a little heap with a glint of red hair'. It wasn't hard to put two and two together, he added.

Frank, the Scholls' son, was the first witness on the second day of the hearing. He told the court that his father had rung him at home in Wiesbaden and said his mum was gone, and so was the dog; the police had already sent helicopters with thermal cameras out looking for them. 'I was amazed they were going to such trouble.'

After a sleepless night he had driven to Ludwigsfelde where his father had been waiting to set out looking with him. They'd been in the woods about an hour. 'The vet was already on his way back when my father called out: "Come over here to the left. She sometimes went this way too." I thought: "What we're doing here is complete madness. The woods are far too big."'

But he walked into the other part of the woods and suddenly came across the shoes, a pair of black slip-ons. 'They were standing there, waiting to be found. My father said: "They're Mum's." I said: "What is this?" I was leaping about like a dervish and he was saying, quite calmly and matter-of-factly: "Yes, they're Mum's shoes."'

The son described how alien his father seemed to him in the days, weeks and months following his mother's death, how quickly he had reverted to everyday life, how little he spoke. He had divided up his wife's jewellery only the day after the funeral and the police later discovered that he'd set aside the bulk of it for himself. In an interview before the trial, Frank had said he wanted to be clear about whether or not his father was guilty. Now, in court, he gave the impression of having long since found the answer.

Heide Sandkuhl's questions, intended to shift the attention away from her client, did little to counter this impression. She asked Frank about calls Brigitte Scholl had received from a stalker, and about a local admirer. She also wanted to know whether he had forwarded letters to the criminal investigation department—personal letters to him from his father.

One of these she read aloud:

Dear Frank,

I can imagine what's going on in your mind. But rest assured that I didn't do your mother and Ursus any harm. I may have been acting a little strangely, because I realised I was the target of police investigations. But I hope I can make up for it some time in the future.

Your Dad

Heinrich Scholl wiped the tears from his eyes, moved by his own words. His son didn't cry. He deflected all attempts to put his father in a better light: the calls from the stalker had been a long time ago, he had only mentioned the admirer to the police so that all possible lines of inquiry could be pursued, and as for the letters, yes, he couldn't deny that he had sent them on. 'The murder squad was my only point of contact. I had to process everything somehow.'

'And did it help you process it?' the defence lawyer asked, coldly.

'I haven't got as far as processing anything yet,' said the son.

His tone too was getting edgier: it was like a long over-due confrontation between father and son, only the father let his lawyer do the talking, and the son stared past them both to the judge's bench. Not once did he look at his father, and the older man too avoided eye contact of any kind. It was like watching some kind of family therapy.

'Have you ever asked your father whether he committed the murder?' the judge asked Frank.

No, he said, he hadn't.

Brigitte Scholl's son returned to his seat beside his lawyer. He was sweating. He looked as if he were returning from battle. In the break he sat with the public prosecutor and the psychiatric expert witness, far removed from the two defence lawyers and his father's friends. The court canteen divided the ranks. Although everyone stood in line together at the coffee machine—prosecutor, defence lawyers, son, journalists, townspeople—once past the till, they split into Scholl supporters, Scholl opponents and neutral observers. Who was on which side often seemed to be a question of belief rather than a judicial question, especially on the days when the hearing touched on all the humiliations Heinrich Scholl had suffered in his marriage.

Like a butler, Gitti had treated him.

He always did what she wanted and never uttered a bad word.

At the end, he'd had to sleep under the roof on a mattress.

The dog had had it better than her husband.

Brigitte Scholl's hairdresser said that Gitti had insisted on getting her own way, even when the hairdresser expressed her doubts: 'Please, Doris! Do it like this!'

Inge Karther wept and laughed as she told the court about the long phone calls between Ludwigsfelde and Anklam.

'When Heiner had to read me the poem,' Maria Zucker reported, 'he said to me afterwards: "She always does that to me."'

'If I told Gitti she was being annoying, she laughed,' said Heike Schramm.

Almost all Brigitte Scholl's female friends continued to come to the hearing even after giving their statements. They wanted to know what would happen next; they wanted to know whether it was Heiner. The trial was as gripping as a crime story—the best entertainment Ludwigsfelde had to offer and, besides, a good opportunity to catch up at last. Since Brigitte Scholl's death, her circle of friends had fallen apart. No one bought theatre tickets any more, no one invited them to the basement bar. Now Heike, Karin and Maria, three energetic pensioners, organised car pools and brought homemade biscuits to the hearing. You could even get used to the canteen food. During Advent there was roast duck and red cabbage; the first week of the new year kicked off with a low-calorie diet from a popular women's magazine. The ladies dressed up for their court visits: trouser suits, blouses, and scarves at their necks. Brigitte Scholl would have been proud of them.

Helga Gerlich, the social democrat from Lichtenrade, used her court appearance to set a few things straight. She had told the police that Frau Scholl always wore the trousers in her marriage, and when the judge asked her what she meant by that, she yelled: 'Somebody has to wear the trousers. I don't know how it is in your household.' She looked defiantly at the judge. When he didn't reply, she gave him a little lecture on women who have to hold everything together. 'We women have the children, we have to do everything and we have to talk till we're blue in the face. I always said to Herr Scholl: "Be glad you have a wife who takes care of you."'

The judge smiled at her as if she were an obstinate child; someone in the gallery groaned. It was one of those moments when you forgot this was about a brutal murder. The unadorned courtroom became a platform for the discussion of major and minor gender issues. How could a marriage end this way? Why had Heinrich Scholl let his wife boss him about so much? And who was actually the victim here?

The women in the gallery were for the most part on Brigitte Scholl's side; the men on Heinrich Scholl's. Among his greatest defenders were his childhood friends. Hans Streck, who hadn't seen Brigitte Scholl since the dress-code fiasco, had been one of the first to visit Heinrich Scholl in custody, and now the trial was under way, he set off on the long trek from his remote village to Potsdam each morning to give his school friend moral support.

Another friend since childhood, the glassblower Dieter Fahle, burst into the hearing in the middle of Frank's questioning. Heinrich Scholl leapt from his seat for joy. For years, Fahle had been living on a sailing ship in Indonesia.

When he had heard that his friend was in trouble, he had jumped straight on a plane. He didn't believe a word of what the prosecutor said. He knew Gitti from schooldays and knew it was his friend Heiner who had been oppressed by his wife, not the other way round. For him there was only one explanation: Gitti had staged her own murder to get one over on her husband. As he saw it, the evidence was unequivocal: Gitti's mother's suicide, her sister's suicide, the funeral plans she had revealed only to her best friend and her son. Last but not least, Fahle claimed that when Frank came to Ludwigsfelde on 30 December, he had brought with him the paperwork setting out his mother's plans for her funeral, even though he couldn't have known she was dead at that point.

In the court canteen, Dieter Fahle's suicide conspiracy theory aroused considerable interest, although everyone agreed you couldn't strangle yourself or cover yourself with moss. But there were so many things that didn't make sense: how, for instance, was Heinrich Scholl supposed to have killed his wife and the dog unaided? Wouldn't Ursus have barked or snapped if someone had attacked his beloved mistress? Why was the corpse covered with moss? What were the shoes doing in the woods? And why would Heinrich Scholl kill his wife in broad daylight and then drive through the town where he had been mayor for eighteen years in a car everybody knew? He was an intelligent man; everyone was agreed on that. He would never have run the risk of being found out.

These doubts seemed confirmed when witnesses were called who claimed to have seen Heinrich Scholl with his wife at the edge of the woods on 29 December, the day of the murder. One of these was Anita Ludwig*, a friend of Scholl's from the SPD. She called him Heiner, knew of his marital troubles and his flat in Berlin. What she didn't know, however, was that he had moved back to Ludwigsfelde. Until, that is, she was driving along Siethener Strasse one day between Christmas and New Year at around midday. As so often when Brigitte Scholl was walking her dog in the woods, Anita Ludwig saw the Mercedes parked at the side of the road. But this time, the mayor's wife was not alone: Anita saw her friend Heiner get out of the passenger door. He was wearing a grey jacket and stumbled as he got out. She said she thought, 'Ooh! Are they back together again?' and then, 'He has gone grey.'

The time of day corresponded with the time of the murder, the place with the crime scene, and Anita Ludwig had precisely recognised the accused. There was only one more question. The judge put it to her with exaggerated casualness, as if to detract from its significance, its force. 'And,' he asked the witness, 'do you remember what day it was?'

Anita Ludwig looked at the judge. Then she launched into a long story about not sending off her Christmas cards on time and having to get it done after Christmas. She had written the cards in the morning and driven to Ludwigsfelde in the afternoon to drop them off at the post office or the news agent's. She had done that on three consecutive days, always between midday and 1 pm. But on which of those days had she seen Herr Scholl at the edge of the woods?

The court heard that on Wednesday, Anita Ludwig had bought a certain variety of potato she particularly liked at the market in Ludwigsfelde. On all three days, she had been to the bank. On Friday it had been her birthday and she'd driven into town twice. She assumed it was on one of these trips that she had seen an emergency vehicle at the edge of the woods. So it couldn't have been Friday. That left Wednesday and Thursday. At her first questioning in January, she had said to herself: 'Wednesday, Thursday, Wednesday, Thursday.' When asked by the superintendent, 'Are you coming down on Thursday then?' she had nodded. Now, in court, Anita Ludwig shrugged. She couldn't remember.

Hers wasn't the only statement to fall apart in court because the witness was suddenly unable to remember exactly what had happened. A cyclist had also seen Brigitte Scholl by her car at the edge of the woods 'with another person'. In her police statement, she had identified this other person as 'Herr Scholl'. Ten months later, in court, the cyclist had changed her story. She hadn't recognised him at the time, she said; she had only reckoned it could have been him.

The next to appear in the witness stand was a gardener who gave her statement in a strange, sing-song voice. On Friday at about twelve o'clock, she had driven to the hyper-market at Langerwisch with her husband. Actually, they only ever went on Tuesdays or Thursdays, she said, but that week it was a Friday, which was unusual. They had seen

Frau Scholl's car. The boot was open, and Brigitte Scholl had been rummaging around in it—'Town shoes off, forest shoes on,' the gardener trilled, making it sound like a nursery rhyme. She had assumed Brigitte Scholl was going for a walk in the woods, as she so often did.

Frau Scholl could not, however, have gone for a walk in the woods on Friday, because she was murdered on Thursday. The gardener's husband clearly recalled that the sun was shining on the day of the murder, but the weather report gave evidence to the contrary. The judge eventually lost his patience, slamming his hand flat on the table. All to no avail. He ended up being told how you know whether a rose is fresh or not: the stem shouldn't be brown at the bottom, the gardener explained.

Though Judge Tiemann usually spoke so softly he could hardly be understood, he had a temper. He exploded if there was talking in the gallery or if the defence asked too many questions. In the breaks, he doffed his robes, put on a leather jacket and went outside for a smoke, looking more like an aging rocker than a distinguished jurist. Brigitte Scholl's girlfriends whispered to each other that Tiemann was 'a dish'.

The confusion and contradictions continued, reaching a climax when Wolfgang Schröder* was called to the stand, a key witness who claimed to have seen Heinrich Scholl in his wife's car on 29 December 2011.

Fifty years ago, Wolfgang Schröder had been the sporty apprentice who cycled from Ludwigsfelde to Teltow every morning and waited on the station every afternoon to take the train back with Brigitte Knorrek. He had been one of her admirers, Heinrich Scholl's rival, so to speak. The man who entered the courtroom on this January day was bald, with a moustache, and a gold chain around his neck. Legs akimbo, he strode to the witness stand. He answered the court's questions with a Russian 'ne znayu' or 'dunno', and some-times he told the judge, 'You just don't get it.' When asked to describe the clothes he'd been wearing on 29 December, he replied drily: 'Waistcoat, cardigan—and trousers, I guess.' The whole courtroom laughed; even the accused and the judge grinned.

Wolfgang Schröder had only seen his teenage sweetheart by chance since her wedding, but he had never lost sight of her altogether. He knew her friends, her dog, her car—and, of course, her husband.

'When did you last see Heinrich Scholl?' the judge wanted to know.

'On the twenty-ninth.'

'Can you tell us about the encounter?'

'I was really stressed that day. The dry cleaners had fucked up my duvet. After that I drove to the dentist to pick up my anti-grinding mouthguard. My appointment was at twelve-thirty; I was out again fifty minutes later. Then I got a few bottles of sparkling wine at Netto and drove off again. On the left, in Fontanestrasse, Gitti's car was parked, and Heiner was sitting in it.'

It was very quiet in the courtroom. Everyone understood

that this was an important statement, perhaps the most important so far.

Who but Brigitte Scholl's murderer could have been sitting in her car?

'Are you sure it was Heinrich Scholl?' the judge asked.

'One hundred per cent sure.'

Everything tallied: place, time, weather. It was not looking good for the accused. Brigitte Scholl's teenage sweetheart was going to be his undoing.

But then, immediately after Wolfgang Schröder, two Ludwigsfelde car dealers testified to having seen Heinrich Scholl at his favourite Italian place at the time of the murder. It must have been 29 December, because that was the day they discovered that their car showroom was to be sold, and they went to Da Toni's as soon as they heard to discuss the situation over red wine. Scholl had been wearing a blue trench coat. He'd approached the restaurant on foot from the direction of the spa, and had also drunk red wine. Until late in the afternoon.

It was a curious statement, above all because Heinrich Scholl himself had never claimed to have been in Da Toni's at midday. His alibi was the spa. After the spa he'd had lunch in Berlin between 2.30 and 3.30 pm. That much was certain; there were witnesses to confirm it.

It was impossible to tell what Scholl made of his double alibi; as usual he was covering his notepad with writing. His lawyer merely asked whether Heinrich Scholl could have been gone for two hours in between times. The witnesses couldn't remember. They stuck to their statement.

It was getting more and more complicated. Everyone seemed to know something, but no one was impartial. Wolfgang Schröder had been in love with Brigitte Scholl. One of the car dealers had once leased an Audi to Heinrich Scholl, and his ex-sister-in-law was a close friend of the accused. Scholl's neighbour had been given lifts to football games and other local events by the mayor. Almost all the men who appeared in court knew Heinrich Scholl from the car works. The women had gone to Brigitte Scholl for facials.

Wolfgang Schröder had to appear in court again a few weeks later because it transpired that the dental practice had been closed between Christmas and New Year; there was also no evidence of the dry cleaning or the purchase of sparkling wine, and the neighbour whom Schröder had allegedly told of his encounter with Scholl claimed to know nothing. No one seemed to take the car dealers seriously any more either. The red wine had flowed freely that day; the court assumed the men had got the day wrong.

The next few days of the hearing were no more enlightening.

The publisher affirmed that she, not Heinrich Scholl, had invented the contentious scene in his erotic tale in which the hero says he's never thought of divorce, but has considered murder.

The police sniffer dog, 'Miss Marple', had followed the trail of a policeman from the crime scene rather than that of Heinrich Scholl.

The mobile phone record, one of the few pieces of evidence that had seemed as if it might hold water, turned out to be unusable: the phone's precise whereabouts at the time Scholl called his friend about their lunch in Berlin could not be proven.

It was true that the traces of DNA found on the underwear and on the shoelace used to strangle the dog very probably came from Heinrich Scholl, but it was hard to say whether they had been deposited when the crime was committed or on a previous occasion in the couple's house. After all, they had shared a bathroom, and it was of course conceivable that the tidy-minded Brigitte Scholl had taken the shoelace with her from home to tie up her bag of moss. Moreover, the sample from the underwear had lain around 'undocumented' at the state criminal police office for a week. The defence referred to this as 'colossal slovenliness' and attempted to take advantage of it by filing an ever increasing number of petitions.

By now it was spring in Potsdam. A long, dark winter was over—the second since Brigitte Scholl's death. Her girlfriends wore brightly coloured dresses and flimsy cardigans. Scholl's friend Dieter Fahle had flown to Indonesia and back. His ship had got caught by a tsunami and been damaged. Sometimes he was accompanied to court by a young Indonesian woman who was looking for work in Germany. She hardly understood any German and didn't even know what her acquaintance's friend was accused of. She smiled a lot, bravely ate the canteen potatoes and was mistaken for

Nantana by the journalists. Dieter Fahle only just managed to intervene when the photographers aimed their cameras at her.

Nantana Piamsuk had appeared as witness some weeks before, a slight, surprisingly unassuming woman in glasses, cloche cap, jeans, shirt and knitted waistcoat. At police questioning she had given 'sex worker' as her profession; in court she looked like a student.

Seeing his former mistress testify was humiliating for the once so highly esteemed mayor. First he had to listen as, coldly and without gratitude, she confirmed the list of his gifts read out to her by the judge; then he had to hear himself described as a sex maniac who had increasingly lost control of himself.

Her witness statement was translated by an interpreter, but occasionally, when she got worked up or thought the accused should be answering the question rather than her, she spoke in German: 'Why don't you ask him?' she asked the judge.

Heinrich Scholl had been jealous and spied on her constantly. 'He said, if you have a new boyfriend, that's fine, if it's nice for you. But his eyes said the opposite. His face was quite pale at that moment. In Thai you say: "He smiles, but he doesn't show what he has in his heart."' Heinrich Scholl, not two metres away from her, listened, pale-faced, his muscles tense, and didn't show what he had in his heart.

She described how she'd grown more and more afraid of him, especially at the end when he had even found out where her new boyfriend lived and broken into her home. Nantana Piamsuk was sure Heinrich Scholl took back the handbag he had given her. An email found on his computer by the police seemed to confirm this. 'As you can see,' he had written, 'I've taken a few things with me. In exchange I'm leaving you our ring.' The email ends with the words: 'Don't worry —I have good people. They'll find you.'

Nantana Piamsuk never read these lines because she had changed her email address. She also immediately deleted the many text messages that Heinrich Scholl sent her. Their content could not be retrieved, but the times at which they were sent were known, and the judge read out those he wished the court to note: 28/12, 11.26 am and 7.07 pm; 29/12, 10.50 pm; 30/12, 12.43 am and 7.54 am. All of these times fell within the days, hours and minutes during which Brigitte Scholl was missing.

It was quiet again in the courtroom. Questions hung in the air, important questions: What had Heinrich Scholl wanted to tell his mistress? That he was free? That he could start a new life with her, without his wife? Who was this man in the dock? Why wouldn't he say what he had thought and done in those last days of 2011? What was he hiding?

Psychiatrist Alexander Böhle, an expert witness appointed by the court, was next to testify. He had spoken at length to Heinrich Scholl in prison and observed him during the hearing from his seat between public prosecutor and Frank. From the outset, Böhle made it clear that there was not much he could say. Heinrich Scholl had, it was true, talked to him about his life, but not about the death of his wife. There was very little material; psychiatric conclusions could only be drawn with difficulty. 'There's a big hole.'

During his first conversation with the expert witness, Heinrich Scholl was politely detached; during the second he was 'more engaged, more open'. He told the specialist 'cheerfully' about his educational and professional development. The accused had been anxious to present himself as a moral, robust and upbeat person, said Böhle; he had—consciously or unconsciously—distorted his answers in order to appear in a better light. A test had shown that Heinrich Scholl avoided direct, aggressive confrontation. 'He doesn't swear back if he's criticised; he suppresses anything like that, or doesn't even register it.' Moreover, because of a huge superego, Scholl tended to accept accusations made by others, turn them against himself and defend himself: 'That wasn't my intention! I didn't mean to!' He had a great deal of trouble with feelings in general and difficulty negotiating emotional relationships. Heinrich Scholl struck the expert witness as 'cold'.

Böhle sees Scholl's childhood as the cause of his problems. He spoke of a 'family background of social and emotional deficiency' and of 'authoritarian structures'. He had, in effect, no father; his mother had been the dominant parent. To this day, Scholl defends her harsh treatment of him, becoming 'really angry' when asked why he put up with so much from his mother. If his mother said something, it was fact. 'A boy who identifies with his mother, a very sad adolescence, a situation in which a child cannot mature much,' was Böhle's conclusion. Such children often grew up into people who misjudged complex human relationships.

His submissive relationship with his mother continued seamlessly into his marriage. 'He went from one regime of dominance to the next,' the expert said. At first, Heinrich Scholl barely noticed, partly because Frank, Brigitte Scholl's son, was treated just the same. Later, Scholl's position as mayor helped him to compensate for his marital problems: 'He was boss then; he had the say.'

Heinrich Scholl, Böhle said, had suppressed his marital problems for decades, denying them and drastically playing them down. He was completely uncritical of his mistress Nantana too, but at the same time 'emotionally very involved'. The relationship was extremely intense on Scholl's side, 'no doubt partly as a result of his desire to catch up; he hadn't had many women'. The expert witness was astonished that a man who had been mayor, and in that capacity had to rely on his 'intuition', a form of emotional intelligence, should completely fail to keep his distance emotionally. But there was no question of a psychiatric disorder or significant psychological abnormality. Heinrich Scholl was of above average intelligence, well able to orient himself and capable of independent reflection. 'Dementia, forgetfulness—all that can be ruled out,' Böhle wrote in his report, 'as can hallucinations, paranoia and schizophrenic psychoses.'

Criminally liable: for the court that was the crucial finding. No mitigation of sentence, then. The psychologist, a

composed man with half-moon glasses and a bow tie, ana-
lysed the man in the dock like a patient. Scholl listened with
interest. Maybe he was comparing the conclusions of the
expert witness with those of his therapist at Lake Tegern.
Maybe he was sorry that Gitti hadn't given marriage counselling with the vicar a real go.

Alexander Böhle described the Scholls' marriage as a
long relationship of dominance and subjugation. Scholl's
inability to show his feelings or let off aggression had led
to a psychosomatic disorder. 'It was more than just a nice
detail that Frau Scholl treated her husband so harshly. There
must have been extreme defence mechanisms in play.' That
would also explain his bowel disease, Böhle said.

When asked whether Heinrich Scholl could have been
the perpetrator, Böhle sketched a possible scenario: Out on
a walk in the woods together, the couple get into a fight. In
the heat of the moment, Scholl strangles his wife. Later, he
'wakes up' elsewhere, returns to the woods, sees the victim
before him, covers her with moss and then calls the police,
'because he can't understand that he did it'. Such things happened, Böhle said. In people as inhibited as Scholl, there was
a particularly high risk of so-called lack of impulse control.

But all that was only a hypothesis. 'I don't know to this
day whether Herr Scholl did it or not.'

Alexander Böhle was the ninety-seventh witness at Heinrich Scholl's trial for the murder of his wife; there followed
further expert and witness statements, including those of
a nine-year-old girl who had been out riding in the woods

with her father and encountered a couple with a dog: Heinrich and Brigitte Scholl. This was the witness found by the vet at the instigation of the accused. Sitting right in front of her, the judge tried to jog her memory with simple questions. In vain. Neither she, nor her sister, nor her father could say what day they had seen the couple.

Witnesses had also come forward in response to the notice in the weekly paper, claiming to have seen Heinrich Scholl at the spa a little after twelve o'clock; that is, at the time of the murder. But it wasn't certain. It could also have been a little before twelve. Brigitte Scholl's death was retreating further and further into the mists of memory.

In his final speech, the prosecutor stuck staunchly to the original charge of heinous murder, citing times and witness statements that matched his version of events. Stefan König spoke next, for the defence. He started by unpicking the prosecutor's chain of circumstantial evidence and then presented his own, according to which Heinrich Scholl could not possibly have been the murderer.

Scholl's second lawyer, Heide Sandkuhl, had prepared her own final speech, in which she made a very different argument, attempting to convince the court that her client had killed his wife in the heat of the moment. If Heinrich Scholl had committed a crime of passion, rather than premeditated murder, he might receive a more lenient sentence. She said she was only doing this in case the court hadn't accepted the first line of argument the defence had presented. This tactical trick was extremely unusual, but Heide

Sandkuhl was very convincing, arguing that an apparently insignificant moment, but one that was wounding to Heinrich Scholl, could have provoked him to break out of his marriage. 'Maybe, in a few highly dramatic seconds, he lost control and exploded.'

Scholl's behaviour after the murder—in the police car in the woods, when he told Ricarda Hoss about the early bloomers his wife had torn up—was, his lawyer said, typical of perpetrators of crimes committed in the heat of passion. 'After the crime, a state of severe shock and bewilderment often sets in; the perpetrator breaks down and can even attempt suicide. A perpetrator who was fully conscious and in control would never have talked like that.' The fact that the dead woman was covered with moss and the perpetrator had attempted to fake a sex offence did not rule out a crime committed in the heat of passion. On the contrary. 'Such behaviour suggests the perpetrator's panicked fury rather than a controlled, calculated act.'

It was not the first time she had appeared in a criminal court, Heide Sandkuhl said in conclusion, but no other recent trial had brought home to her with such force how hard it was to reconstruct the truth.

Frank's lawyer began his final speech with the words: 'The defendant's son has been through one of the hardest years of his life.' He ended by saying: 'The co-plaintiff pleads for conviction for manslaughter. The prison sentence should on no account be less than ten years.' Frank was silent. In the break, afterwards, he said that it had been the little things in particular that had convinced him of his father's guilt. That on the night of the murder he had parked his car in the garage where his mother's Mercedes was usually parked. That he had moved straight back into the bedroom she had banished him from. That he had inquired of all sorts of neighbours and friends about his wife, instead of ringing home from time to time. Not a single call had been made to the landline of their house on the afternoon of 29 December. For Frank the answer was clear: his father knew that his wife was not going to return home.

It wasn't until after the final speeches, when the judge offered him the last word, that Heinrich Scholl got up from his chair. He had kept up his silence for seven months, listening to what others had to say about him, his wife and his marriage. 'I can only assure you once again that I did not kill my wife and our dog,' he said. His voice was husky; he spoke quickly, without pausing. 'I have tried, in these fifteen months I've spent in custody, to prove my innocence, with the few people and means at my disposal. Because I knew I couldn't find witnesses who would incriminate me. Thank you.'

It was a protestation of innocence, no doubt about it, but it was so awkwardly worded that it sounded almost like a confession of guilt.

Four days later, everyone came together one last time, for the verdict: the defendant's son, his cousin, childhood friends, business partners, Brigitte Scholl's girlfriends, the superintendent, police, neighbours, townspeople, legal reporters from all over the country. It was a warm sunny day in May. One spectator turned up in a straw hat, as if to an outdoor concert.

In the cluster outside the courtroom, the sentence was discussed. Murder, manslaughter, acquittal. The majority gravitated towards manslaughter; almost nobody reckoned with murder. Three of Heinrich Scholl's friends had come to collect him from the back of the courthouse in case of an acquittal. His childhood friend Hans had prepared a room for him in his house in the country; even the bed was made up. His friend Dieter wanted to take him to Indonesia on his ship as soon as it was seaworthy again. An old business friend with good contacts in America was likewise on standby.

When Heinrich Scholl entered the dock, he was wearing a grey pin-striped suit and the polo shirt from the first day of the hearing. In his hand he held a yellow exercise book, which he placed on the table in front of him.

As the judges entered the courtroom for the last time, the spectators rose from their seats. 'In the name of the people,' said Judge Tiemann, 'the accused Heinrich Scholl is sentenced to life imprisonment for murder in coincidence with the killing of a vertebrate animal without reasonable cause. He is to bear the costs of the proceedings and the expenses incurred by the co-plaintiff.'

Heinrich Scholl swayed back and forth; for a moment, it looked as if he would fall over. The sentence had been delivered, the trial was over.

Nearly over.

The reading of the judgment went on for four and a half hours. The judge went a long way back, describing Heinrich Scholl's marriage, the couple's strained relations, Brigitte Scholl's unwillingness to change, her husband's life in Berlin, his pathological jealousy, his attempts to win back his mistress and the precipitate return to his wife. For the judge, Scholl's return home was clearly part of a plan: 'He was entertaining the idea of killing his wife.'

There followed a disquisition, delivered quietly and impassively, on Scholl's behaviour before, during and after the crime. Only occasionally, when taking issue with the arguments of the defence, would the judge raise his voice: 'What rubbish!' He accused Scholl and his lawyers of seeking to influence witnesses with the notice in the weekly paper. 'The accused hoped that people who had seen him in and around the spa before twelve o'clock on 29 December would come forward and erroneously allege to have observed him in the time between 12 am and 1.10 pm.'

What angered him most were allegations that the police had fixed on Scholl too quickly. It was, he said, no wonder some witnesses had said something different at the trial from what they had told the police: 'They were worried about incriminating Herr Scholl. No one could imagine that he had killed his wife; he was the former mayor of Ludwigsfelde, an honourable man. And yet here in the courtroom you often get to know sides of a person that no one could previously have conceived possible.'

Scholl's lawyers left the courtroom. A spectator unwrapped her sandwiches. Finally, Judge Tiemann closed the hearing with a weary wave of dismissal. Heinrich Scholl sat slumped in front of his exercise book.

He hadn't written a word.

LIFELONG

Driving to see Heinrich Scholl is like travelling to the end of the world. You pass through deserted villages until you come to one of those thinly populated towns that are abandoned by the young because they can't find work there. You drive along broad main roads, past industrial ruins, and eventually, when you've almost come out at the other end of town, you turn into a side road, leave your car in a large car park, and walk past an end-of-the-line tram stop, a boarded-up clubhouse and a Soviet army tank until you come to a concrete fortress surrounded by high walls and barbed wire.

The prison in Brandenburg an der Havel was built in the thirties, at about the same time as the Ludwigsfelde munitions factory where Heinrich Scholl's father found work. Nazi resisters were locked away here: communists, social democrats, dissident academics and artists. Erich Honecker spent eight years here as young man, imprisoned by the Nazis for high treason, before being freed by the Red Army and going on to become a dictator himself, leading East Germany for nearly two decades. Another prominent inmate was Horst Mahler, a founding member of the Red

Army Faction, also known as the Baader-Meinhof group. Initially an extreme leftist, Mahler subsequently became one of the most dangerous right-wing extremists and Holocaust deniers in the country.

History is complicated. Lives are complicated. The prison is a reminder of that, an unintentional monument.

Heinrich Scholl is sitting facing the wall in a corner right at the back of the visitors' room, two plastic bottles—Coke and fizzy apple juice—on the table in front of him, and a bar of Ritter Sport chocolate left over from the previous visit. Dieter Fahle has just been, the friend with a boat at anchor in Indonesia. An acquaintance from Berlin was supposed to be coming too, but it looks as if she's changed her mind. 'Not many come now,' says Heinrich Scholl.

It is a day in late May, two weeks after the verdict. His lawyers have gone straight to appeal, but that does nothing to lift his mood. Heinrich Scholl feels let down. His childhood mates remain loyal, but he no longer hears from his powerful politician friends. When he was the model mayor from the East, they liked to be seen with him. Now he's in trouble, they have dropped him. A few days after his conviction, a letter came from the SPD with no salutation; only a subject line: 'Immediate action against Heinrich Scholl'. The party executive were notifying him that internal proceedings had been initiated, because of 'severe damage to the party's political standing and credibility'. 'Prompt intervention' was called for. It made no difference, the letter informed Heinrich Scholl, that he had been involved and active in the party in many ways over the years.

The party he had helped to found in Brandenburg was ashamed of him. It was almost as much of a blow as the judge's verdict. Only two days ago had Heinrich Scholl summoned up the strength to reply. 'Dear Sir/Madam,' he wrote, 'Although my verdict is not yet final, I would like to avoid any further damage to the party and hereby resign my membership of the SPD with immediate effect. I apologise for the dishonour I have brought on the SPD.'

He meant it ironically, but after posting the letter, it occurred to him that it sounded more like a confession of guilt.

It was a year and four months ago that he was arrested. Since then he has been sitting in the remand prison, fluctuating between despair, self-pity and pugnacity. It is only here in prison that he has woken up to what he's lost—not just his wife, but his son too, his whole family. He says he doesn't know how it could have come to this—he didn't do anything to deserve it—and there have been times when he's thought about ending it all. But then, almost in the same breath, he starts to talk about his old exciting life or the appeal his lawyers are working on. He laughs and cries. One moment, he's as bitter as an old man; the next, he's as high-spirited as a boy.

He often talks about his son. Long before the trial began, Frank visited him in prison for the last time. He doesn't call or write any more either. Their lawyers are negotiating the sale of the house in Ludwigsfelde. At the thought of the house, tears well up in Heinrich Scholl's eyes: the lovely house, his garden, his fireplace, his barbecue. All lost.

They had such a good relationship in the past, he says. He never referred to Frank as his adoptive son; he always looked after him. Frank had such a lot to thank him for. Heinrich Scholl shakes his head, uncomprehending, disappointed, and lists all the charges Frank brought against him in court, commenting on them, correcting them, criticising them. That he and his lawyers didn't show Frank any documents, for instance—simply not true, he says. 'I managed to bring the indictment out here into the visitors' room so that he could read it. Don't ask how. But Frank wasn't interested; he didn't even want to look at it.'

Or the scene in the woods on New Year's Day when he got out of the car and bent down, and his son thought he was planting evidence: it was a mouse! He saw a mouse! A dead mouse! In court, Heinrich Scholl kept silent. Now it comes bubbling out of him—all the injustices and injuries he has had to bear in silence. Heinrich Scholl stares at his hands, and when something particularly annoys him, he thumps on the table top. The police were biased—*bang*. The judge locked him up—*bang, bang*. Witnesses claimed things that weren't true—*bang, bang, bang*.

He understood that his wife wanted the grave to herself, but it hurt him terribly that he didn't find out until after her death. 'No one told me anything about it. If I'd known, I wouldn't have moved home. I thought Gitti wanted me to come back. The way I wanted to come back. I lived my life in Berlin, but at the weekends I always had a real yen to go home.'

When you've been listening to Heinrich Scholl for a while, you have the impression that the whole world—and not least his dead wife—conspired against him. After her death he had tidied her cupboard and found a sex toy. He lowers his voice: 'Why would I put a condom and a Viagra pill in my wife's pocket?'

Then who did?

He shrugs and says he doesn't want to accuse anyone when he's not sure. 'I know what it's like to be wrongly convicted.'

What does he say to his friend Dieter's suicide theory?

Heinrich Scholl sits up and breaks open the bar of chocolate. 'I have my doubts,' he says, in professional tones, as if he were back in his office in the town hall. 'Someone would have had to do it for her. You can't strangle yourself, and she was punched twice in the face as well. Mind you, I'd like to have read whether she had anything in her system, any drugs, or poison of some kind, before she was strangled—or whether she was maybe even dead before her body was hidden in the forest. There must have been a struggle, but it didn't necessarily take place where she was found. Because the report says there were signs of dragging—or, at least, that they looked for them. Who on earth goes so deep into the woods?'

It's a strange moment; it is hard to know what to say. Is this an ice-cold murderer and a liar speaking? Or is it a madman? Or a victim of the justice system? Heinrich Scholl makes for a very convincing innocent.

'I never hurt her—that is to say, never consciously,' he says. He refers to his flat in Berlin and his affairs as 'my lone wolf thing'. Such compromises are just a part of life, he says, and they go on all the time. 'If I'd wanted to hurt her, I could have shouted and sworn and carried on. But I didn't. I respected that woman all my life. We were a functioning family. We didn't fight.'

You can suppress a murder, psychologists say, just as you can suppress other terrible things that happen in your life. On the other hand, you always have to remember precisely what you have done if you are to avoid making a mistake, saying the wrong thing, giving yourself away.

The psychiatric expert Alexander Böhle had reported at the trial on how Heinrich Scholl managed to play down problems when he saw no other way out: his mother's coldness in his childhood, his powerlessness to react to his wife. Denial and suppression were always part of his survival strategy. Whatever you talk to him about—his relationship with his son, his time at the circus, his career as mayor—you end up with the impression that he's always made a success of everything. Scholl paints a rose-tinted picture of his life. It is deeply unsettling when he boasts about his marriage—or praises Ursus, the spaniel. He says he misses Ursus, although witnesses testified that Heinrich Scholl never liked his wife's dog. He sings Nantana Piamsuk's praises too, as if he's forgotten his anger, bitterness and misery at the course their relationship took, and what she revealed about him in court.

Scholl spends his time reading books and watching television programs about innocent people wrongfully convicted, living behind bars. He is fascinated by the methods judges use to make their decisions in circumstantial trials, and obsessed by Franz Kafka's famous novel *The Trial*—the grotesque tale of a bank employee who is arrested out of the blue one morning and eventually executed without having found out what he is accused of. Scholl says it reminds him of his own fate. He ought to stop reading these books, he says, or his hopes of a positive ruling at the appeal hearing will dwindle yet further.

He affirms his innocence to everyone he writes to: his childhood friends, his former deputy in the town hall, his colleague from Paderborn. 'I had nothing to do with Gitti's murder,' he writes. Or: 'Rest assured that I didn't kill Gitti and our dog.' Most of them believe him. They consider Heinrich Scholl far too clever for such an amateurish murder. Or they simply can't imagine him capable of killing anyone. Dieter Fahle is still convinced that Gitti somehow pulled the strings herself, and dreams of taking the case to the European Court.

Three months have passed since the trial ended, and Heinrich Scholl grows more belligerent with each visit. The documents supporting his appeal are complete now, and the bound file is as fat as a book. The first hundred pages deal with the errors made by the expert who evaluated the DNA samples, and with all the petitions filed by the defence that were subsequently rejected. Next, the witness statements that the court had cobbled together into a chain of circumstantial evidence are taken to pieces. The defence argues that the chain holds together only if it is accepted—as the court asserted—that at least eleven of the witnesses had made errors in their testimony.

In the final third, the pace picks up. At issue is a letter that wasn't mentioned in court, although it could have put a completely new slant on the case. The letter—sent to Heide Sandkuhl in May 2012—is anonymous, like those that had informed Brigitte Scholl her husband was cheating on her. But Heinrich Scholl is not the one accused of an affair this time. According to the anonymous writer, Brigitte Scholl had a relationship of many years with the husband of one of her friends. No one knew about it, not even the friend, the letter says. 'Gitti wanted to come clean and make the affair public in 2011, and it proved to be her undoing.'

In other words: her lover is alleged to be the murderer.

Heinrich Scholl was informed about the letter and its contents, and said he was not surprised to hear his wife might have had a lover. In June, Heide Sandkuhl put the letter in the court files—because it was anonymous, it was of little value to the defence. There it was found by Scholl's son and his lawyers, who checked the handwriting against the letters of condolence and soon identified the letter writer. Frank had known her since childhood; her mother had been one of Brigitte Scholl's customers. It wasn't clear how this woman came to be so well informed about Brigitte Scholl's love life, but Frank and his lawyer wanted to leave that to the court to find out. They added the handwriting sample to the files, and there it remained. No one paid it any attention, and no one considered it necessary to inform the defence. It was only after the verdict that Scholl's lawyers discovered that the letter's author had been identified.

Heinrich Scholl knows the woman who wrote the letter. She and her mother sometimes came to the naturist bathing spot in the eighties, and to fireside evenings at the Scholls'. He hasn't seen her for a long time.

So how did she know that Brigitte Scholl, who never revealed anything to anyone, was having an affair?

Heinrich Scholl shrugs.

He knows his wife's alleged lover. The man visited him in custody after the arrest, and so did his wife. They now know about the accusations. If you ask the man about it, he says there's nothing in it. His wife doesn't know what to say. First her friend was murdered, then her friend's husband was arrested and now her own husband is supposedly involved too. The two of them suspect that someone commissioned the letter, trying to shift the blame. They feel used by Heinrich Scholl. It's a very long time since they last went to see him in prison.

The mysterious correspondent no longer lives in Ludwigsfelde. None of Brigitte Scholl's friends knows who she is; no one can remember her or her mother. There is only her anonymous letter and the note of condolence to Frank. She did enclose a telephone number, but when you dial it, the phone just rings. No one answers. Perhaps she knows that she's been identified and that her letter could have an important role to play in an appeal. If it comes to an appeal. It is not very likely. As a rule it is not the facts of a case that are assessed in an appeal, but only whether formal errors were made in the course of the trial. The chances that the trial will be reopened are not particularly high in any case. In recent years the number of successful appeals has hovered just under ten per cent.

It will be several months yet before Heinrich Scholl learns the outcome of his appeal. One day in February 2014, he will hear on the midday news that it has been dismissed, but no reasons provided. The verdict will be final then, but for now there is still hope. In the meantime, he has no choice but to resign himself to prison life.

The first person he got to know in the remand prison was Axel Hilpert, a man around his age—Scholl was then seventy, Hilpert five years younger. Like Scholl, Hilpert was something of a legend in Brandenburg. In the old days, he had been an unofficial Stasi informant and an antiques buyer; after the collapse of the Wall, he switched to property. Together with Jochen Wolf—the minister who later hired a hit man to kill his wife—he was involved in a dodgy construction business. He was sentenced to five years and eight months' imprisonment for serious fraud, breach of trust and tax evasion in connection with the development of a luxury hotel complex. Hilpert's lawyers were filing an appeal against the sentence.

Hilpert's cell was diagonally opposite Scholl's in a newly renovated part of the prison. The corridors there are wide; the kitchen is tiled; there are no bars at the doors. Hilpert showed Scholl where the kitchen was and where you could get clean laundry. He knew the ropes; he took him under his wing. Scholl could talk to him and ask his advice. Hilpert introduced him to the editor-in-chief of the inmates' newspaper and supported Scholl when he first thought of placing an ad in the weekly paper looking for witnesses who could provide him with an alibi.

Their cell neighbours were considerably younger—and tougher. They were all members of the Hells Angels—musclemen with thick necks, shorn skulls and tattoos all over their bodies. They cracked jokes about large Hilpert and little Scholl and had their fun with them.

Heinrich Scholl loves to tell the story of how they poured salt in his coffee and he drank the whole cup without batting an eyelid. When Bullet (whose real name is Steffen) said, 'Hey, Scholl, wash my floor,' he told him he needed to sweep it first. Scholl laughs as he relates this tale. He can assert himself, even today. That's what he's trying to prove with these stories. He's a leader, even here in jail.

Recently he asked Kay, another of the Hells Angels, for a cigarette in the yard, triggering a fight about the dangers of smoking. The upshot was that Kay pointed at the rainwater in the ashtray and said other people drank that kind of thing. Bullet asked Kay whether he'd give Scholl a cigarette if he drank the brew.

'Not just one, a whole carton,' Kay replied. He didn't know that his fellow inmate had once bitten the head off a mouse—or that he had climbed the world's highest peaks.

Heinrich Scholl put the ashtray to his lips.

When Axel Hilpert was released on bail due to concerns about his health, Heinrich Scholl was left with the bikers. The bikers had been sentenced to several years' imprisonment by the same judge as Scholl and, like him, were going to appeal. That bonds them. They call him 'Scholli'. He calls them 'my boys'.

They cook together, play skat, and go to church every other week. Heinrich Scholl likes the peace and quiet there, and the talks with the vicar. The bikers mainly go along for the free coffee and biscuits after the service. Scholl lifts weights with them, and until recently they also played football together. Heinrich Scholl plays well, but the guys from Brandenburg knock him flying without even realising. Now he prefers to jog round the yard—alone.

After a few months they'd had to move out of the new block into the old one. 'Appalling conditions,' Heinrich Scholl says, 'like in Sing Sing.' He cleaned the toilet with his toothbrush, it was so filthy. In summer it was forty to fifty degrees Celsius in his cell. Sometimes he thought he couldn't hack it any more: the long corridors so narrow you can't even pass someone coming the other way, the jangle of the keys at the guard's waist, the scrape of the lock every morning at half past five when they check on him in his cell to make sure he's still alive. When Heinrich Scholl had to have an operation in the prison hospital, he hoped he wouldn't wake from the anaesthetic—that he'd simply go to sleep and be free of all his worries. He's thought seriously about suicide. 'Twice I almost ended it,' he says. 'Twice I came close to seeing the bright light.' But he's stopped 'any of that'. His lawyers have told him that suicide would be tantamount to confession. That's given him the courage to carry on living. There'll be no confession of guilt from Heinrich Scholl—never.

In late October 2013, a year after his trial first started, Heinrich Scholl makes his way to the visitors' room. He is wearing an old pair of jeans and a faded jumper—his work clothes. First shift and lunch are already over. In the summer he took care of the flowers round the prison yard; now that autumn has come round again he's got a new job as an editor at the prison newspaper, where he writes pugnacious articles railing against the bad food and the expensive goods on sale in prison, and speaking up for inmates' rights. He also contributes short stories and articles on the German judicial system. In some editions he has three articles. His editor-in-chief—a graphic designer doing time for the murder of a Thai woman—is pleased with his new, motivated colleague. Heinrich Scholl's friends joke that he'll soon be running the prison.

He gets on better than ever now with the Hells Angels, especially Bullet, the one with the most tattoos, the thickest muscles and a voice as rough as sandpaper. When Heinrich Scholl mentions him, his voice becomes fond, almost tender.

He talks about Bullet's difficult childhood: his mother didn't want him; he was sent to a home and later to adoptive parents; the father beat him. Bullet was sentenced for brutally beating another biker, but Heinrich Scholl believes him when he says he didn't do it. He's amazed that Bullet's turned out such a good lad. With that childhood! Heinrich Scholl knows what he's talking about.

Bullet is like a son to him, now that he's lost Frank. Scholl's lawyers have found a letter in the files in which Frank congratulates the court on its excellent work and thanks all involved. Heinrich Scholl lays his son's letter on the small table in the visitors' room and presses his lips together.

His mistress fled from him, his wife is dead, his son has turned his back on him. Heinrich Scholl is as alone at the end of his life as he was at the beginning.

Without Bullet and his friends in prison, he would hardly have survived. They have become a new family to him. They protect him from the other inmates; he helps them with their official documents. When Bullet puts his heavy arm around his shoulders and says, 'Hey, Scholli, can you have a look at this letter for me?' it makes his day. He likes helping, he says; he always did. His eyes grow moist; he turns his head away. When he has collected himself, he says: 'Since being here, it's become clear to me that I haven't actually made any fundamental errors in my life—that I've only done good. Even the love I bought myself—that's much better than starting a relationship with a woman and getting her hopes up. I have nothing to reproach myself with. I don't want to talk myself into thinking there's anything I could have done better. I've fathered offspring, planted trees, written a book, been up the highest mountains in the world. I've already done the fundamental things in my life. I just don't want to end it here.'

Scholl has taken up painting again. He's brought one of his pictures along to the visitors' room: a lake in front of a setting sun, a backdrop of mountains and, in the foreground, a couple sitting on a bench under a tree. The motif isn't his; he copied it from a postcard, the way he used to when he was a boy and had to earn money after school for his mother.

It looks as if Heinrich Scholl is starting over from the beginning.

THE CLASS REUNION

When Brigitte Scholl began to organise her class reunion in the summer of 2011, she was adamant that it should be the last. Soon after the Wall came down, she had met up with her schoolmates from Ludwigsfelde High School for the first time. That was when she had just turned fifty. Now, twenty years on, she was approaching seventy and that alone was reason enough for Brigitte Scholl to decide there wouldn't be another reunion. She thought of seventy-year-olds as elderly people who talked only of their ailments—a nightmare for the woman who had once been the class beauty. She wanted her schoolmates to have good memories of her.

Siegfried Schmidt, who helped with the preparations, saw things differently. He would have liked to carry on a few years longer with the class reunion. But there was no persuading Brigitte Scholl. She was the self-appointed organiser-in-chief; the one who set the agenda, made the appointments, invited their former teachers and drew up the program. Dinner in a restaurant was not enough; there had to be something special as well: a visit to their old school, a tour of the town, a tour of the Mercedes works. Her husband usually came along too.

Heinrich Scholl would be standing at his wife's side at the arranged meeting place, even though he wasn't one of her class. He was guest of honour and tour guide in one. The time before last, in 2009, a tour of the new naturist spa was on the schedule. Heinrich Scholl distributed white plastic slippers to Brigitte Scholl's classmates to put on over their shoes. They walked along the galleries, pretending not to see the stark naked spa guests at the edge of the pool.

At the last reunion, in October 2011, Heinrich Scholl was not there. He was originally supposed to have taken Gitti's class around the local heritage museum, but she had discarded that plan without explanation and asked a colleague of his from the town hall archives to give the tour instead. Heinrich Scholl was instructed by his wife to show her friend Inge's husband around Ludwigsfelde, but instead he had driven him to Berlin to show off his flat—and the lingerie in the bathroom.

Such last-minute changes did not bode well, you might think, but the final reunion proved to be the best of the lot. Brigitte Scholl sat among her old classmates, laughing with the women, flirting with the men, like in the days when she was fifteen, a girl with a petticoat and a ponytail. Out on the street, she took Inge by the hand and danced along the pavement with her. She seemed more carefree than she had for a long time. Maybe that evening with her old schoolmates, she sensed for the first time that she could make it alone. Life went on.

The next morning she rang Siegfried Schmidt and told

him she'd changed her mind: there would be another reunion, in two years at the latest. It would be best if they started to organise it straight away. Siegfried Schmidt was surprised at Brigitte Scholl's change of heart, but what really astonished him was her drive. She rang almost daily to discuss the details. She even fixed the day, time and place: 17 October 2013 at 4 pm in the 'Old Inn'.

On 21 December 2011 they spoke on the phone for the last time. Siegfried Schmidt thanked Brigitte Scholl for the bottle of wine and the Christmas card she had left at his front door. 'Dear Siegfried,' the card said, 'Thank you on behalf of all your schoolmates for going to so much trouble to organise the class reunion for us. Merry Christmas, Gitti.'

Siegfried Schmidt kept the card. For him, it was more than a Christmas greeting: the card was a mandate.

It is 4 pm on the dot, 17 October 2013, a bright sunny autumn day. Outside the wooden houses on Rathenau Strasse, Michaelmas daisies are in flower. In the woods of Ludwigsfelde, mushroom gatherers are out in force. Siegfried Schmidt stands at the head of a long table and welcomes his schoolmates to the seventh reunion of the Class of 1951. Everyone has come, even if there was slight confusion about the time they were to arrive. Siegfried Schmidt had written '3 pm' on the invitations, but after sending them off, he had come across the slip of paper where he had jotted down the essentials of Gitti's reunion plan. 'Start: 4 pm,' it said. Plain and clear. He changed the invitations and sent out new ones. From behind the scenes, a dead woman was directing.

It was as if the Scholls were still playing their old roles. Heinrich Scholl was making a name for himself again, this time in prison. Brigitte Scholl was keeping everything under control.

There is no guided tour; instead there is a visit to the cemetery. Brigitte Scholl's class lay a flower arrangement on her grave: a cushion of flowers and moss with a bow saying: 'Thinking of you. Your classmates.' The evening's guest of honour is Frank, Brigitte Scholl's son, who has come from Wiesbaden especially. He misses Siegfried Schmidt's speech, but is in time to hear the others. Frank is touched by how well they all speak of her—not one bad word—and by the autumn table decorations, which are just as his mother would have liked them. Siegfried Schmidt has gone to particular trouble over the commemorative book. It is even thicker than the last one. The front cover shows the old school in Ludwigsfelde and, superimposed on it, another photo, a large portrait of a dark-haired woman in a white jumper.

Brigitte Scholl is smiling.